Family Child Care Curriculum

Also by Sharon Woodward with Donna C. Hurley

The Home Visitor's Manual: Tools and Strategies for Effective Interactions with Family Child Care Providers

FAMILY CHILD CARE CURRICULUM

Teaching through Quality Care

SHARON WOODWARD

Redleaf Press®
www.redleafpress.org
800-423-8309

Published by Redleaf Press
10 Yorkton Court
St. Paul, MN 55117
www.redleafpress.org

First edition 2011
Cover design by Jim Handrigan
Interior typeset in Adobe Garamond Pro and designed by Mayfly Design
Interior illustrations by Todd Balthazor
Printed in the United States of America
17 16 15 14 13 12 11 10   1 2 3 4 5 6 7 8

Library of Congress Cataloging-in-Publication Data
Woodward, Sharon.
   Family child care curriculum : teaching through quality care / Sharon Woodward.
        p. cm.
   Includes bibliographical references.
   ISBN 978-1-60554-012-2 (alk. paper)
   1. Family day care—Activity programs. 2. Early childhood education. 3. Child development. I. Title.
   HQ778.63.W662 2011
   362.71'2071—dc22
                        2010011086
Printed on acid-free paper

For Philip, Jamie, Michael, and always, David—
my most rewarding learning experience

Contents

Preface

There is no question that family child care is an important profession. It is the uniqueness of family child care that allows me to feel so much excitement about welcoming you to *Family Child Care Curriculum: Teaching through Quality Care.* For years, many providers have shared their frustration that child care resource materials do not reflect the reality of a family child care setting. There are many books for child care centers, where there are generally more staff, more space, and greater resources. In quality family child care programs, the smaller group size, multiple ages of children, and home-based setting favorably approximate a child's experience at home. When questioned, many parents say they chose a family child care placement because it does feel more like home. But as states revise their licensing requirements, including more emphasis on more structured and age-appropriate curriculum, the multiage children and informal home environments that have traditionally defined family child care can sometimes create a challenge. The challenge may occur when a provider attempts to introduce curriculum that meets the developmental needs of multiage groups of children with limited staff and restricted available space. As a result, the primary goal of *Family Child Care Curriculum* is to offer creative ways for providers to meet age-appropriate developmental objectives for all the children in a typical family child care setting. This book includes realistic strategies for you to use with the children you care for.

During my twenty years as a family child care licensor, I had the remarkable opportunity to visit thousands of family child homes. The diversity of my caseload allowed me to license family child care programs in urban three-room apartments, large suburban homes, and almost everything in between. I have had the pleasure to observe excellent programs operating in all types of environments. In creating this book, I have attempted to include the best practices and innovative ideas that I have observed. In developing this curriculum, the objective has always been to create a reader-friendly resource specifically for family child care providers. This curriculum provides activities that can realistically be used with multiage groups and easily included in your daily routine.

My experience in child care is not limited to licensing. I also owned and operated a large child care center, in addition to being a parent who purchased child care for all three of my children. As a result, I have looked at child care from three different perspectives. While operating my center, I was convinced that center-based care was the most positive setting for young children in child care. In looking back, I can say without hesitation that I was foolishly biased. I assumed that individuals working in centers were better trained and better able to provide an appropriate setting for young children.

All of that changed when I had my first child. After much consideration, my husband and I placed our infant in a family child care home. In retrospect, I am convinced our decision was the best one for our family. Not only was our son in a loving, warm, and stimulating environment, but as first-time parents we were better able to go to work each morning without feeling massive amounts of guilt. My son's family child care provider allowed us to experience, firsthand, the wonderful benefits of her personalized and professional care. Our son flourished, and my respect and newfound appreciation for family child care grew by leaps and bounds.

As I began working as a family child care licensor, I occasionally encountered situations that broke my heart, situations that sometimes occurred as the result of the death or the serious injury of a child. Nonetheless, I quickly became aware that the large majority of home businesses I visited were amazingly well run. Programs that came in all shapes and sizes were organized to allow every child, regardless of age or developmental stage, to benefit. As a result, I found myself developing a deeper respect for the family child care profession. It was that very respect and those impressions that inspired me to begin what I called my family child care journal. That journal became the inspiration for this curriculum.

This book was written to acknowledge all the wonderful — and in some cases miraculous — things you do on a daily basis. My hope is that you use this book frequently and that in some small way it helps you in your very important job.

Acknowledgments

Thank you to Frances and Daniel Brunelle, who always told me I could.

Thank you to Donna Hurley and the Bethel Child Care staff for their encouragement and support throughout the development of this curriculum guide.

To Paul Hughes, who continued to support and encourage me even when I was ready to throw in the towel.

To Georgia Gray, supervisor, and Jean Wilson, licensor, my former colleagues at the Office for Children. Thank you for your thoughtful and intuitive insight regarding family child care.

To Kyra Ostendorf and David Heath and the rest of Redleaf Press, who gave me the courage and support to create this curriculum.

Finally, to you, the family child care providers who invited me into your homes and demonstrated the true meaning of quality child care, thank you.

Introduction

Teaching through Quality Care

As we learn more about how young children learn and grow, it becomes increasingly apparent that a quality family child care program can and should have a lasting effect on participating children and their families. Quality family child care provides children with education and loving, continual care. It is the best of both worlds. In that spirit, the objective of this curriculum is to demonstrate how multiage groups of children in family child care can be taught through quality of care.

Very often the word *teach* brings to mind a formal learning setting. But children begin to learn from the moment of birth. Children learn from what they see, hear, and do. As a result, you are teaching during every interaction that occurs in the course of the day. In providing quality care to young children, it is impossible not to teach. Children learn by watching, listening, and attempting to replicate your behavior. Child care, with an emphasis on the word *care,* has to include all the components that allow for healthy development. A provider who has developed effective and creative learning activities, but neglects to change diapers when needed, is not providing quality child care. Successful family child care programs have the best organization of space and time. Maximizing all the points of contact during a typical family child care day provides an opportunity to meet all the early child care curriculum objectives. The word *curriculum* as it applies to family child care generally means a method of instruction. Curriculum objectives (what a curriculum should accomplish) in early child care include understanding several developmental domains.

- Physical and Motor Development: a child's growth and how he or she develops the large muscles for walking, running, and throwing, and the small muscles for drawing, writing, feeding, and dressing.
- Social Development: how a child interacts with other children and adults by sharing, cooperating, and following rules.
- Emotional Development: a child's self-esteem, self-control, and ability to express feelings.
- Language Development: the ability to listen, understand, speak, and eventually to read and write.
- Cognitive or Intellectual Development: a child's ability to think, reason, solve problems, form concepts, remember ideas, and recognize objects.

Developmental domains are the specific areas of learning that young children need to grow and develop. Part 1 includes an overview of each learning domain from birth through age five: physical and motor, cognitive, communication and language, and social and emotional. I also include a detailed list of developmental milestones from which this curriculum was built. It is important that each domain be addressed in your daily schedule of activities. The activities in this curriculum are creative and inclusive to allow for the healthy development of the infants, toddlers, and preschool children who participate in your family child care program.

How to Use This Curriculum

The foundation of a successful program is the relationships you have with the children in your care, which allow you to know their individual needs to support their growth and development. The nonmobile infant is given space to stretch on a blanket. Then, as a baby working on crawling, she is given encouragement and room to move. When this same baby is ready to pull up and try walking, you provide sturdy furniture and a soft landing spot to support and encourage this new phase of development. Later the toddler needs safe but challenging places to climb, and the preschooler needs room to run and kick a ball. The same series of development occurs with cognitive, language, and social/emotional learning. Providing safe challenges and encouragement facilitates the learning that young children need to grow and develop. This curriculum has been organized to support this type of teaching through quality care.

Family Child Care Curriculum is designed to be as reader friendly as possible. The material is organized to use as a reference so that you can find what you need when you need it. Units 1 through 4 provide an overview of typical child development by developmental domain:

- Unit 1: physical and motor development
- Unit 2: cognitive development
- Unit 3: communication and language development
- Unit 4: social and emotional development

Each domain is divided into age groups to facilitate planning for the learning that occurs for children in your care. A chart of developmental milestones shows the typical age range when each milestone is met. The curriculum's activities are built from these milestones. For example, there are activities designed to promote eye-hand coordination, a physical development milestone.

Unit 5 is an overview of how to set up your program and evaluate your practices. It provides tips on creating learning environments and safety concerns to be aware of. Creating a nurturing and safe environment is an important part of preparing for the children. Setting up materials ahead of time allows you to be organized and free to participate when you and the children start an activity.

Unit 5 also describes the importance of partnering with the families of the children in your care. Parents and guardians are each child's first teachers, and as such, they deserve your respect. Communicating your philosophy and approach and building a relationship with each child's family is key to a successful experience for the children in your care. Families who are confident of your abilities will send children who are more willing and eager to participate and learn. This unit offers suggestions to help make the transition between the child's home and yours as smooth and seamless as possible.

Part 2, the activities, is the heart of this book. It opens with a description of how to identify learning objectives and choose activities that will support and challenge each child. The activities that follow are divided by learning domain and then by content. There are five content areas within the domain:

- Use Senses
- Explore Movement

- Interact with People
- Interact with Toys and Objects
- Develop Verbal Skills

Within each content area, the activities are presented by age level. This allows you to choose an activity based on the needs of a specific child or two while incorporating the other children in the same or similar activities.

The illustrations in part 2 are designed to help you recognize which content area and age group the activities connect to. There are fifteen illustrations, one for each age group and content area:

Use Senses

Infants

Toddlers & Twos

Preschool Children

Explore Movement

Infants

Toddlers & Twos

Preschool Children

Interact with People

Infants

Toddlers & Twos

Preschool Children

Interact with Toys and Objects

Infants

Toddlers & Twos

Preschool Children

Develop Verbal Skills

Infants

Toddlers & Twos

Preschool Children

Many of the activities are designed to complement the tasks and routines that are part of each family child care day. Activities have also been developed to easily complement the overall goals of a quality family child care program:

- healthy physical development for all the children
- age-appropriate cognitive development
- opportunities for the development of good language and communication skills
- creation of an environment that enhances social and emotional development

The activities in this curriculum purposefully encourage you to be an interactive participant. This is an especially important component in family child care, where commonly only one adult is present. The most necessary prerequisite in providing quality child care is your willingness to actively participate in the program. Regardless of how expensive or how abundant the materials and equipment, the happiest and best-adjusted children are in the homes of providers who are the most directly and consistently involved. Cost-effective and easily implemented activities that allow you to interact with each participating child enrich your program.

The activities are designed to capitalize on the available space in a traditional home-based setting. This is important. Perhaps one of the most dramatic changes in family child care in the past ten years is the growing trend to create settings that replicate center-based environments. Many providers have additions or converted basements, or have turned over large sections of their living space, all with the intention of creating settings much like those one might encounter in a child care center. One reason providers do this is to accommodate additional children and generate more income. Other providers have expressed the desire to maintain their competitiveness with child care centers while feeling this type of renovation is the only method available to them. Ironically, these types of changes have occurred during a period when many centers are simultaneously attempting to create more intimate and cozy settings, or less "institutionalized" child care environments.

The most successful family child care programs are located in homes where providers have chosen materials and activities that complement the uniqueness of their environments. Good management of space and time are essential in the operation of a thriving family child care business. When writing your schedule of activities, though, it is important to assess whether chosen activities can realistically be implemented in your environment. You may find, for example, that water and sand table activities are not realistic in your setting. If not, your challenge then becomes determining what sensory activities can be included. There is always more than one way to accomplish a developmental objective. For example, sorting socks for color and texture, playing with dough or shaving cream, and finger painting provide wonderful sensory experiences. There are many opportunities for children to engage in water activities that do not require a water table. Attempting to force a square peg into a round hole is not only frustrating but also rarely successful. Creating a curriculum that meets the developmental needs of all the participating children, while allowing providers and their families to enjoy the character of their homes, should not be mutually exclusive goals.

Following the activities is a collection of information that applies to all age groups. This information reflects frequent questions from family child care providers, including information on using computers with children, having pets in your home, and caring for children with food allergies, as well as safety information. I include book and Web site resources you can use to inspire your teaching through quality care.

Caring for Infants, Toddlers, and Preschool Children

This curriculum acknowledges all the beneficial interactions that occur between a caregiver and children and provides suggestions on how those contact points can be maximized and made even more meaningful. Knowing that learning occurs as a result of your involvement in the daily tasks that are a normal part of quality care will assist you in identifying your role in caring for the children and should help you to make adjustments, as necessary, to capitalize on all the meaningful moments that occur naturally and spontaneously.

Infant Care

The infant activities reflect the research about how and when babies learn. Since family child care providers may care for a child from early infancy to kindergarten, establishing a good beginning is very important.

To support the huge amount of growth and development that occurs in infancy, the infant activities are subdivided into three age groupings: birth to six months, six to twelve months, and twelve to eighteen months. Information about expected outcomes is included with the activity information. This information will also assist you in evaluating your infant program. A sample daily schedule for infants is included.

Toddler Care

The word *toddler* is used throughout the curriculum to refer to children ages eighteen to thirty-six months. Children this age generally have limitless energy as well as an enormous amount of curiosity, and they are often fearless. The toddler activities provide general information about toddler development while incorporating physical and motor, cognitive, communication and language, and social and emotional development.

Information will allow you to understand the expected outcomes for each activity. The curriculum also includes information that will assist you in evaluating your toddler program. A sample daily schedule of activities is included.

Preschool Care

For children to progress and to begin school ready for formal instruction, thoughtful preparation must occur on the part of the early childhood professionals. Family child care providers are certainly not exempt from this responsibility. The preschool activities for children ages thirty-six to sixty months include general development information in addition to developmental goals covering the learning domains.

Establishing a formal preschool environment within a family child care setting is not always possible. The curriculum provides information about how to create a viable preschool area in your home while incorporating age-appropriate activities and achieving expected outcomes. Suggestions for forming collaborative partnerships with parents and community resources to allow preschool children a smooth transition from child care to a more structured school setting and a sample daily schedule for preschool care are included.

Part 1

Understanding the Needs of Children

Getting to know each child and understanding developmental benchmarks that apply to each child help you to include activities that correspond with each child's developmental stage. With a variety of activities and materials at your disposal, you will have many options as you plan your daily schedule of activities.

Typically developing children grow and develop in similar patterns. However, every child is an individual. The following information is simply a guideline for growth and development. As you will note, a range of ages is included in the developmental milestone information. If you have concerns regarding a child's development, you need to communicate your concerns to that child's parents or guardians. As a child care provider, you have a unique opportunity as well as a very real responsibility to tell parents what you see, hear, and feel about the healthy development and well-being of their children while in your care.

Unit 1

Physical and Motor Development

Physical development describes children's growth, while motor development refers to their ability to move their bodies in a coordinated manner. Motor development includes small- and large-muscle (or fine- and gross-motor) skills, which are described below.

Good physical development begins with good eating habits. Healthy neurological development in infants, as well as healthy growth and development in older children, starts with proper nutrition. In addition to good nutrition, physical activities that promote large-muscle development for all age groups are necessary and important parts of any family child care's daily schedule. Running and jumping, throwing and catching, walking and skipping are all necessary components. It is important to remember gross-motor skill development is necessary for infants as well as older children in your program. Exercises and games that provide for large-muscle development in infants will assist in their ability to roll over, crawl, and eventually take their first steps.

Developing small muscles, as well as fine-motor skills, is an equally important goal. Coloring, cutting, and turning the pages of a book are all examples of daily activities that promote healthy motor development. Motor development is as necessary as all the other curriculum objectives and should never be overlooked. Planning a successful daily schedule of activities must include the opportunity for active and robust play. Appropriate scheduling and good utilization of available space, both in and out of doors, is necessary in accomplishing this important objective.

Infant Physical and Motor Development

Between birth and eighteen months of age, children experience an incredible amount of physical development and motor skill improvement. An infant who begins by tracking movement with his eyes and reaching for a finger is soon sitting up and grasping small toys. Little fingers that begin by grasping your finger are quickly grasping a bottle and just as quickly grasping a cup. Legs that initially kick and stretch are soon crawling and eventually taking those first wondrous steps.

Infants Birth–6 months

Physical development before six months of age usually includes learning to push up from the floor and roll over. Infants need time during the day to lie on their stomachs on a blanket on the floor or outside on the grass. Sit in front of them and encourage them to push up.

Kicking develops motor skills and is something that comes naturally to infants. Use many of the activities included in this unit to encourage this type of activity. Given the opportunity, infants love to wiggle themselves all over the place. These wiggles and shuffles are preparing them to crawl. Place infants on their stomachs and lie on the floor facing them as frequently as possible. Use the suggestions in this book as well as your own creative ideas to encourage infants to shuffle forward. Offer an enthusiastic response as infants work hard developing these motor skills.

Help infants roll over from their stomachs to their backs to promote necessary muscle development. Put infants on their stomachs on a soft, flat surface. As you plan your day and create objectives for each child, remember to include sufficient time for infant activities that promote physical development.

Infants 6–12 months

Small- and large-motor skills develop separately. For example, an infant at six months may be able to sit in a high chair without support but not be able to grasp small objects until seven or eight months of age.

Infants in this age group should be given ample opportunity to sit supported when necessary and to sit unsupported when appropriate. Six to twelve months of age is also the time when most infants begin to crawl. Activities that encourage this skill should be included throughout the day. Ample protected space provides opportunity for infants to move and play. When establishing your daily schedule, look at ways you can offer a variety of activities for multiage groups in an area where you can adequately supervise all the children. Create an open and safe space for infants on the floor near an activity table where older children are working. This allows you to supervise both age groups while allowing infants important opportunities for physical development.

During this developmental period, infants are also beginning to grasp objects and transfer toys from one hand to another. You will want to assure you have sufficient infant materials that are safe and sized appropriately for small fingers to grasp and experiment with.

Infants 12–18 months

Infants in this age group are walking, so it is important that your environment adequately provide for this developmental milestone. Infants should be encouraged to walk when they are ready. It is your job to assure your child care setting is hazard free. Children in this age category can usually walk unassisted and will, if allowed, cruise around the available space, sometimes holding on to furniture for additional support. Look at your space and assess how best to place low furniture, which can provide assistance in this important activity. Make sure stairways are protected by gates, because these infants will try to climb stairs. Some providers incorporate supervised stair climbing as an effective infant activity. When the infant climbs the stairs, the provider follows, always closely supervising. This allows the infant to exercise both leg and arm muscles and stay safe while climbing.

Small-motor skill development for older infants often includes activities such as placing one block on top of another or scribbling with crayons. While the infants need to be supervised carefully during these activities, it is important that these types of opportunities be offered to them in addition to the other children in the group.

Toddler Physical and Motor Development

Physical development is extremely important to the overall healthy growth and development of toddlers (eighteen to thirty-six months). Toddlers walk alone, and usually by two years of age they run with a large, if somewhat awkward, gait. Children in this age range are usually able to jump and ride small tricycles with or without pedaling. When scheduling your daily activities, be sure to include opportunities for activities that promote coordination and balance. Look at your indoor and outdoor space carefully. Are you accommodating these activities and others while promoting good physical development throughout the course of the day? Most toddlers prefer large-motor activities, such as running, jumping, kicking, dancing, pedaling, pushing, pulling, throwing a ball, and participating in simple but active games. This strong desire for large-motor skill development begins as toddlers' coordination improves.

Fine-motor activities should also be encouraged to ensure the refinement of small-muscle coordination. Building towers with blocks or other stackable materials, turning the pages of a book, and moving their fingers independently are examples of developing fine-motor skills. Ample opportunity for these types of activities should be available, because eye-hand and fine-motor skill development play a huge part in a child's ability to prepare for future learning. Having small-motor skill materials (books, crayons, scissors, blocks) available to toddlers is a must.

Preschool-age Physical and Motor Development

Preschool children are generally taller, thinner, and more adultlike in their appearance than infants and toddlers. Three-year-olds enjoy repeating physical activities, such as sliding, jumping, or riding a bike. Three-year-olds can usually walk on a balance beam or hop on one foot. They can bounce and catch a ball. They love to run, and they do so frequently without falling. Three-year-olds are learning to draw simple shapes; zip; snap; and fasten; and use scissors, brushes, pens, pencils, crayons, and markers. Usually at this stage their toilet training is completed.

As the three-year-olds grow and their gross-motor movements develop and mature, their ability to run, jump, hop, throw, and climb should continue to improve. They begin to dress unassisted and to run with ease. They can put puzzles together.

Older preschoolers begin to use the left or right hand predominantly. You need to permit children to use their preferred hand comfortably. That means your environment must accommodate left-handed children as well as right-handed children. Baseball gloves and left-handed scissors are examples of accommodating left-handed children.

Proficient use of scissors is another important developmental milestone because it shows that five-year-olds are developing their pincer grip, the small muscles in their hands that allow them to hold a pencil. Opportunities for this type of development need to be considered in each day's schedule of activities for preschoolers.

Understanding these benchmarks means that as part of your quality care, you make sure you have sufficient and appropriate materials to foster all of these types of healthy physical development. Preschool children need outdoor space where they can engage in gross-motor activity, as well as effectively organized indoor areas that provide them with ample opportunity to refine their fine-motor skill development.

Physical and Motor Milestones

Infant Physical and Motor Development Milestones

Milestone	Generally Begins
Reacts to loud noises	Birth–2 months
Moves head from side to side while on stomach	Birth–2 months
Brings hands to face	Birth–2 months
Focuses on objects 8 to 12 inches away	Birth–2 months
Turns head to both sides while on back	2–3 months
Follows moving object with eyes	2–4 months
Holds head steady when carried or held	2–4 months
Brings hands to midline while on back	3–4 months
Rotates or turns head from side to side with no head bobbing	3–4 months
Plays with hands and may hold and observe a toy	3–5 months
Reaches for objects	3–5 months
Follows distant object with eyes	3–6 months
Rolls over	4–6 months
Lifts head while lying on back	4–6 months
Brings feet to mouth easily while lying on back	4–6 months
Holds up chest with weight on forearms	4–6 months
Attempts to crawl (stomach and legs dragging)	5–9 months
Grasps small objects	6–8 months
Transfers object from one hand to another	6–9 months
Can be pulled to feet but can't support self	6–9 months
Gets to sitting position/sits unsupported	6–9 months
Accepts being spoon-fed	6–9 months
Crawls (trunk lifted)	6–11 months
Cruises (walks around holding on to furniture)	9–12 months

(Continued)

(Continued)

Milestone	Generally Begins
Walks with assistance	9–12 months
Stands alone	10–15 months
Walks alone	11–18 months
Scribbles with crayon	12–15 months
Uses small muscles in hands to squish playdough	12–15 months
Crawls up and down stairs	12–18 months
Enjoys clapping hands	12–18 months
Begins to exhibit fine-motor control, such as using a spoon	12–18 months
Puts one block on top of another	12–18 months

Toddler Physical and Motor Development Milestones

Milestone	Generally Begins
Walks up and down stairs with help, usually leading w/same foot	18–24 months
Runs with large gait	18–24 months
Throws a ball	18–24 months
Feeds self	18–24 months
Begins to dress self	18–24 months
May begin toilet training	18–24 months
Builds tower of three or more blocks	2–2½ years
Runs with ease	2–2½ years
Stands on tiptoes	2–2½ years
Hammers	2–2½ years
Turns pages of book one at a time	2–2½ years
Jumps from height of 12 inches	2–2½ years
Moves fingers individually and draws circle	2½–3 years
Rides tricycle—may alternate between scooting and pedaling	2½–3 years

Preschool-age Physical and Motor Development Milestones

Milestone	Generally Begins
Copies and draws simple shapes	3 years
Can use scissors	3 years
Uses small muscles in hands to color, cut, paste, and paint	3 years
Swings arms when walking	3 years
Walks on a balance beam or line	3 years
Balances or hops on one foot	3 years
Jumps into air with both feet	3 years
Slides without assistance	3 years
Throws a ball overhand	3 years
Bounces a ball and catches it	3 years
Runs consistently without falling	3 years
Builds and stacks with several small blocks	3 years
Practices zipping, snapping, fastening, and buttoning	3 years
Makes marks or strokes with drawing tools	3 years
Begins to stay dry while sleeping	3 years
Naps less frequently	3 years
Completes toilet training	3 years
Walks up and down stairs, alternating feet	3 years
Dresses with little assistance	4 years
Runs with ease and stops quickly	4 years
Throws a ball overhand with greater accuracy and distance	4 years
Pedals and steers preschool-sized three-wheelers with ease	4 years
Scoots on two-wheeled bike without pedals and/or pedals and steers a two-wheeled bike with training wheels	4 years
Puts puzzles together with ease	4 years
Uses large muscles to throw, climb, skip, hop, jump, catch, turn somersaults, and bounce	4 years
Writes own name	4½ years

(Continued)

(Continued)

Milestone	Generally Begins
Throws a ball to a target overhand and underhand	5 years
Catches a ball when thrown or bounced	5 years
Balances well	5 years
Uses left or right hand predominantly	5 years
Jumps over objects 8 to 10 inches high without falling	5 years
Kicks a ball with accuracy	5 years
Begins learning to jump rope	5 years
Begins learning to tie shoes	5 years
Rides two-wheeler	5 years

Unit 2

Cognitive Development

Cognitive or intellectual development describes a child's ability to reason, think, and solve problems. Activities that promote forming concepts, remembering ideas, and recognizing objects are all appropriate and necessary curriculum activities in child care. To teach young children effectively, it's necessary to understand their individual needs as well as their abilities. A structured learning activity that involves construction paper, glue, and cotton balls, for example, may be an appropriate activity for a toddler or preschooler, but not for an infant. There are, however, many activities included in this curriculum that will enhance cognitive development in infants.

The expression "Play is children's work" stems from the fact that so much of intellectual development in young children can be accomplished through supervised play. It is important to introduce activities for all children during the day that provide for intellectual development through creativity and exploration.

Infant Cognitive Development

For infants, cognitive development describes the way in which they begin to understand their world. Infants come prewired to communicate their needs almost immediately. They cry when they are hungry, wet, or in need of comfort. The way in which you respond to them should provide positive feedback. Infants will learn to hold a bottle, shake a rattle to produce noise, suck efficiently, and seek out a ball that has rolled out of sight. Infants depend on feedback to understand how to navigate their world. How do their caregivers respond when they cry? What happens when they grasp a bottle in a specific way? What is the result when they shake a rattle? These are all examples in which infants need feedback to grow and develop cognitively. All of these examples of learned motor behaviors illustrate what Jean Piaget called the *sensorimotor* stage. Piaget believes that intelligence is the ability to adapt to one's environment. Piaget's theory includes what he refers to as the six developmental substages within in the sensorimotor stage covering the first eighteen months of life.

The first substage, from birth to one month, involves innate reflexes, such as sucking movements. The second substage, two to three months, involves the repetition of simple acts—opening and closing of fists and repeatedly fingering a blanket. The third substage, four to six months, contains more intentional activity: kicking a leg in order to produce a swinging motion in a toy suspended over the crib, for example. In the fourth substage, seven to ten months, infants begin to solve simple problems: for example, move a pillow in order to find the toy partially hidden behind it. During the fifth substage, eleven to eighteen months, infants begin to show trial and error experimentation. An infant who has learned to pull the pillow with his hand to find his toy may now try to kick a pillow down to achieve the same result. At this stage, infants generally attempt to repeat and prolong activities they enjoy. These infants are beginning to understand the variation of movements and events they can initiate on their own. Substage six, which is the most advanced stage, generally occurs around eighteen months and involves imagining or inventing events before acting them out in reality. Understanding how infants develop cognitively allows you to better plan activities that contribute to and reinforce their development.

Infants Birth–6 months

The idea that infants cry simply to exercise their lungs is simply not true. As you care for infants, it is important to recognize that just because you may not understand the reason behind an infant's cry doesn't mean there is not a legitimate reason for it to occur. When an infant in your care is crying, he is trying to communicate his needs. It is important to respond with care to determine the reason for the crying.

Infants in this age group explore their environments using their eyes, ears, and sense of touch to accommodate the fact that they are not yet mobile. They will turn their heads toward sounds and touch. You can effectively support and reinforce this sensory behavior by providing appropriate stimulation and responding to their cues.

As infants near six months of age, allow them to choose from a variety of grasping toys. You will note that usually these infants are grasping and holding on for longer periods of time.

Infants 6–12 months

Having safe and sufficient materials for infants in this age range is important. These infants are beginning to explore cause and effect as well as trial and error. They are more inclined to manipulate objects for a desired outcome or result. Safe equipment with buttons and levers that produce sounds are beneficial at this developmental stage. Offering a variety of materials, including rattles and age-appropriate grasping toys, promotes healthy cognitive development. Remember that infants will mouth all the toys and materials they use for exploration and play. Be watchful about choking hazards and diligent about appropriate sanitation.

Infants 12–18 months

Infants in this age group are on the move and want to explore everything. Language development overlaps with cognitive development when older infants start talking—they can and do say no. They also wave good-bye without a prompt and can tell when objects still exist although they seem to disappear (a toy underneath a blanket, for example). Games and activities that reinforce these cognitive behaviors in positive ways are important. Playing peekaboo and building block towers are two ways that safely challenge older infants and support cognitive development.

Toddler Cognitive Development

Within Piaget's four stages of development, toddlers are now entering the preoperational stage. This stage continues to age six and involves developing the ability for egocentrism and conservation. Egocentrism, in this definition, is the inability to separate one's own thoughts and beliefs from other people. Conservation, on the other hand, is the ability to decipher what changes and what stays the same after a physical transformation. For example, if the same amount of liquid is poured into two different shapes of cup, can the child tell that it's still the same amount of water? Toddlers are learning during every interaction, so you are teaching during every interaction. Successful family child care providers teach by giving children useful information and positive examples. As toddlers develop the skills to give verbal feedback, it becomes easier to evaluate their individual needs. Their ability to verbalize also means an increased obligation for more verbal participation from you. For example, when presenting toddlers with your schedule of activities for the morning, identify each activity chronologically. "First we will hang up our coats; then we will have breakfast. After that, we will have group time." This allows toddlers to learn about time and organization of thought and action and to develop vocabulary and language skills. Toddlers ask questions and expect them to be answered. "Now" and "Why?" are favorite words of many toddlers. Talking with toddlers and answering questions in an understandable and patient way are important in fostering cognitive development.

Toddlers want to touch and explore everything they can see, hear, or smell. Everything is a new experience. You may think young children know what they can and cannot touch. In reality, this is commonly untrue. Every touch produces a new sensation. A toddler who is constantly being told "no" and "Do not touch" is not being taught but denied opportunities to learn. Be sure your child care environment allows for free and safe exploration.

Preschool-age Cognitive Development

Cognition includes thinking, remembering, problem solving, imagining, judging, and deciding. All of these skills develop in conjunction with language development. During the preschool years, children develop their ideas of cause and effect, space, velocity, objectivity, and time.

Three-year-olds are beginning to notice differences, and they are beginning to discover patterns and textures in the environment. In evaluating your materials and equipment, it is especially important to include activities and games that promote this important type of development. As preschoolers grow and develop cognitively, they ask a lot of questions. It is not uncommon for their sentences to begin with *who, what, where,* or *why.* As with toddlers, there always needs to be sufficient time and patience to respond to preschoolers' questions. When preschoolers are responded to positively and come to understand that their questions and comments are welcomed, they will feel more comfortable and confident about verbalizing their feelings. As preschoolers mature, you will note that they are often thinkers and doers, especially when enriched environments with lots of concrete activities stimulate their brains.

Cognitive Milestones

Infant Cognitive Development Milestones

Milestone	Generally Begins
Appears to know that crying will bring attention from caregiver	Birth–2 months
Prefers black-and-white or high-contrast patterns	Birth–2 months
Explores environment with senses	2–4 months
Discovers hands and feet are extensions of self	2–4 months
Responds to own reflection in mirror	2–4 months
Anticipates events	2–4 months
Shows interest in manipulating toys and objects	4–6 months
Investigates objects by banging, shaking, and throwing	6–9 months
Shows interest in objects with moving parts	6–9 months
Shows interest in playing games	6–9 months
Responds to "no, no"	9–12 months
Waves bye-bye	9–12 months
Shows awareness of object permanence (knows objects exist when out of sight)	9–12 months
Engages in more intentional play	9–12 months
Intentionally selects toys to play with	9–12 months
Shows understanding that objects have purpose	9–12 months
Follows simple commands from adults or older children	12–18 months
Enjoys books, especially turning pages	12–18 months
Tracks a moving toy and retrieves it when partially hidden	12–18 months
Practices cause and effect, such as closing doors	12–18 months

Toddler Cognitive Development Milestones

Milestone	Generally Begins
Recognizes own image in mirror	18–24 months
Recognizes colors	18–24 months
Pretends to read	24–30 months
Can do simple sorting	24–30 months
Names some colors	24–30 months
Repeats simple nursery chants and rhymes	24–30 months
Sings parts of simple songs	24–30 months
Shows an interest in shapes	24–30 months
Engages in more pretend play	24–30 months
Uses the word *no*	24–30 months
Talks about books	30–36 months
Can tell own age	30–36 months
Knows first name	30–36 months
Recalls past experiences	30–36 months
Asks questions	30–36 months
Creates imaginary friends	30–36 months
Follows more complex directions from adults	30–36 months

Preschool-age Cognitive Development Milestones

Milestone	Generally Begins
Names simple shapes	3 years
Recognizes own name in print	3 years
Shows an interest in numbers and names of numbers	3 years
Can stay with the same activity for five to ten minutes (increasing concentration)	3 years
Uses props to symbolize real objects	3 years
Engages in fantasy play	3 years
Puts interlocking puzzles together	3 years

(Continued)

(Continued)

Milestone	Generally Begins
Identifies and names body parts	3 years
Uses positional terms	3 years
Begins to notice patterns	3 years
Can sort or describe objects by one or more attributes	3 years
Uses real objects as props during pretend play	3 ½ years
Uses words for time, such as *yesterday* and *today*	3 ½ years
Is developing memory skills	3 ½ years
Begins to reason	4 years
Sorts or categorizes	4 years
Engages in more developed play themes	4 years
Understands simple concepts, such as age, number, and distance	4 years
Puts things in order or sequence	4 years
Counts objects out loud	4 years
Shows interest in the alphabet	4 years
Is developing early literacy	4 years
Counts twenty or more objects with accuracy	5 years
Sorts and organizes	5 years
Uses measurement terms	5 years
Understands the words *whole* and *half* and uses them in sentences	5 years
Matches objects with ease	5 years
Knows some names of coins and bills (money)	5 years
Estimates numbers in a group	5 years
Draws basic shapes and expressive art	5 years
Expresses interest in creative movement	5 years

Unit 3

Communication and Language Development

Communication and language development refers to a child's ability to physically and verbally share information and to listen or see and understand information from other people. These abilities eventually allow a child to read and write. Talking with and encouraging children to express their ideas while listening and valuing what they have to say may seem like ordinary, everyday occurrences. In reality, these occasions are very important parts of your daily schedule. Interacting with and engaging children in conversation are essential elements in any successful child care curriculum. A quality family child care program provides opportunities for children to express themselves interactively in a safe and receptive environment. The dialog that takes place at arrival time, during group or circle time, at the lunch table, or while you read a book are examples of when language skill development occurs. Talking and listening are cost-free daily activities that can easily be applied to all the age groups in your program. In looking at your daily schedule of activities, remember to allow sufficient time for conversation. Doing so will only enhance each task and activity.

Infant Communication and Language Development

Infants are born communicators. In the first few weeks of life, crying is an effective way of getting needs met, because a baby's needs are limited to food, sleep, and comfort. As the infant matures and begins to seek attention, cooing begins to take the place of crying. Coos eventually give way to other sounds, and those eventually become words. An important part of your job is to get to know each child well enough to identify verbal and nonverbal signals. All children communicate in a variety of ways. Your personalized knowledge will allow you to respond to each child's needs before words are possible.

One of the most valuable interactions you have with infants is conversation. Each day needs to include the opportunity for providing words, listening, and encouraging infants' vocalizations. If the day becomes so scheduled that there is very little time for talking and listening, something is not right. Children entering grade school with the ability to effectively express themselves are well on their way to a successful learning experience. Developing this competency begins in infancy. All activities need to provide sufficient time for talk.

Infants Birth–6 months

Do infants use language? Many providers and parents say that infants make themselves understood. For example, an infant's cry when wet may be very different than the cry she uses when she is hungry. In truth, infants cry for a variety of reasons. They may cry because they are in pain or because they are cold or overstimulated. Infants may also cry because of a lack of physical contact. Infants frequently employ their own types of body language when attempting to communicate their needs. Some infants will toss and turn their heads when tired or hungry. Other infants will make shapes with their mouths to signal hunger or discomfort. As you become increasingly familiar with each infant in your care, you will become increasingly aware of individual communication signals. Paying close attention will help you to respond to signals, which in turn will encourage infants to communicate their needs.

Infants listen to speech and are most responsive to the human voice. At two or three months, they can usually be soothed or quieted by their caregiver's calming voice. By the second half of their first year, they may understand their name and the names of some of the things around them. Because of this, the sound of your voice and the repetition of your words are especially meaningful.

Changing a diaper, feeding, or washing infants provides great opportunities for conversation. You can gain the attention of the youngest infants by gently touching an arm or leg. Use their names as frequently as possible. While you are accomplishing a task, talk about what you're doing—for example, "Now your diaper is clean," "Just a minute and I will get your bottle." When babies gurgle or coo, gurgle and coo back. Repeating sounds helps infants begin to learn language.

Infants 6–12 months

Infants in this age category are beginning to accidentally and then consciously imitate sounds. In most instances, they will respond to simple directions, such as "Show me your ear" or "Where is Daddy?" Infants in this age range are also beginning to call some people by name, such as "Mama" or "Dada." Keep in mind that talk is not only an important but also a cost-effective learning tool. Even infants who are barely verbal can participate in conversation. Encourage their response, even when that response is limited to coos. Take the opportunity whenever possible to engage infants in conversation. Talk about what they are able to see while sitting in their high chair or crawling on the floor. Give names to objects, and talk about what you are serving for lunch—for example, "Look at these orange carrots" and "This is a green bean." Use words as frequently as possible. Occasionally you might assume that because infants don't speak, they are not interested in your speech. This is not true. Talk frequently and expressively. When speaking to infants, remember to use their names.

Infants 12–18 months

Infants in this age category usually have a vocabulary of anywhere from three to fifty words. They really speak for the fun of it and do not generally exhibit a lot of frustration if they are not easily understood. If you haven't already, you should be introducing simple stories and nursery rhymes as well as repetitive songs. Infants in this age group are beginning to demonstrate how much they enjoy those types of activities. Remember that engaging them and providing positive reinforcement for all their communication attempts are important parts of any effective infant curriculum.

Toddler Communication and Language Development

Toddlers can usually communicate in short sentences and understand most of the things you say to them (receptive language skills). They can become very frustrated if you do not understand what they have to say (expressive language skills). The best way to foster communication and language development is practice, practice, practice. As you proceed through each day's tasks and activities, talk with the children.

Vocabulary development is based on exposure to words. As toddlers become more confident when speaking, introduce a larger variety of words. Describe out loud what you are doing as you are doing it, and encourage the children to describe what they are doing or observing throughout the day.

As their skills increase, many toddlers enjoy reciting short poems, nursery rhymes, and songs. Encourage this type of activity frequently. Reciting rhymes while bouncing a ball, for instance, is a wonderful way to promote language development as well as eye-hand coordination. With increased vocabulary comes a willingness to interact more in conversations. Toddlers are sometimes able to recall sequences of events, so ask them what they did over the weekend or invite them to retell a favorite story. Older children love this activity because it allows them to prompt the toddlers when necessary. Some children at this age may stutter because they think faster than they can speak. It benefits all children when you listen patiently as they struggle to express themselves.

Preschool-age Communication and Language Development

Three-year-olds explore words and the power that words have when used in certain ways. Unlike younger children, preschoolers will usually speak to you when you have spoken to them. They will tell you stories without being prompted to do so, and they like learning new words. Rather than being taught words, preschoolers like to imitate you and will repeat the words you use. Young three-year-olds can speak in three- or four-word sentences, while older three-year-olds can use up to seven words in a sentence. Three-year-olds are beginning to use correct grammar. Consequently, it is important that you use good grammar when speaking with them.

As preschoolers age, their vocabulary increases and their language improves. You will notice that when preschoolers reach five years of age, their language skills grow by leaps and bounds. Five-year-olds will speak in six- to ten-word sentences that are sometimes nonstop. Five-year-olds will also argue and reason while using the word "because" frequently. By the time they are six, children should be able to talk to adults easily, and they generally ask a lot of questions.

Providing language opportunities for preschoolers is especially rewarding. Engaging in more in-depth conversations with children is a tangible demonstration of the effectiveness of your family child care curriculum. Confidence is a great attribute as children move forward. You enhance preschool children's ability to move to more formal learning environments when you emphasize language development. Speaking, listening, reading, and writing are all interrelated. What children hear, they can say. What they say, they can write. What they write, they can read. Language is not taught effectively in isolation; it is more successful when integrated into daily activities. Encourage children to describe their block structures, how they feel during dramatic play, their art work, and their comprehension at story time. A total-language approach will also help children grow intellectually, socially, emotionally, and physically.

Communication and Language Milestones

Infant Communication and Language Development Milestones

Milestones	Generally Begins
Reacts to human voice and human heartbeat	Birth
Cries when hungry, tired, overstimulated	Birth
Coos in response to adults' speech	1–2 months
Makes squealing and gurgling sounds	2–4 months
Babbles consonant sounds, such as "da-da-da"	4–6 months
Laughs out loud	4–6 months
Babbles sounds, such as "goo" and "gaa"	6–9 months
Experiments with vocalizations to include longer and more varied sounds	6–9 months
Uses intonations in sounds	6–9 months
Responds to own name	6–9 months
Develops receptive-language vocabulary	6–9 months
Says at least one word	9–12 months
Gestures or points to communicate	9–12 months
Listens to songs, stories, or rhymes with interest	9–12 months
Imitates sounds	9–12 months
Uses gestures and actions intentionally	12–18 months
Intentionally says "mama" and/or "dada"	12–18 months

(Continued)

(Continued)

Milestones	Generally Begins
Uses one sound to stand for more than one gesture or object	12–18 months
Speaks in jargon or nonsense phrases	12–18 months
Understands many more words than can be expressed	12–18 months
Understands and responds to simple directions	12–18 months
Has vocabulary of three to fifty words	12–24 months

Toddler Communication and Language Development Milestones

Milestone	Generally Begins
Says "hi," bye," and "uh-oh"	18–24 months
Begins to express feelings with words	18–24 months
Uses two- to three-word phrases	18–24 months
Shows an interest in print and books	2–2 ½ years
Begins to use private speech	2–2 ½ years
Shows ability to use naming words for objects of interest	2–2 ½ years
Puts nouns and verbs together in simple sentences	2–2 ½ years
Echoes questions	2 ½–3 years
Uses understandable speech	2 ½–3 years
Uses a loud and soft voice	2 ½–3 years
Has vocabulary of more than 300 words	2 ½–3 ½ years
Understands most things said by others	2 ½–3 ½ years
Responds to things said by others	2 ½–3 ½ years

Preschool-age Communication and Language Development Milestones

Milestone	Generally Begins
Uses up to seven words in sentences	3 years
Likes to learn new words	3 years
Asks many questions	3 years
Speaks when spoken to	3 years
Tells stories without prompting	3 years

(Continued)

(Continued)

Milestone	Generally Begins
Begins to use correct grammar	3 years
Understands the meaning of most preschool words (semantics)	3 years
Uses language socially (pragmatics)	3 years
Enjoys singing simple, repetitive songs	3 years
Enjoys books and has a sense of how books work	3 years
Listens for details	4 years
Follows three-step directions	4 years
Uses appropriate speech (rarely uses baby talk)	4 years
Speaks in seven- to ten-word sentences	4 years
Sings more complicated songs; enjoys fingerplays and rhymes	4 years
Retells a simple story in sequence	4 years
Refers to yesterday and tomorrow correctly	4 years
Pronounces words and sounds correctly	4 years
Uses pronouns in sentences	4 years
Spells name	4 years
Answers questions about familiar stories	5 years
Argues, reasons, and uses "because"	5 years
Makes up stories	5 years
Asks lots of questions	5 years
Converses easily with adults	5 years
Uses language to control	5 years
Has an expanding vocabulary	5 years
Speaks clearly and fluently, constructing sentences that include details	5 years

Unit 4

Social and Emotional Development

The term *social and emotional development* describes how children learn to interact with other people and understand their own and others' emotions. Self-regulation—the conscious and unconscious ability to control your actions so you can function with others—is an important component of social and emotional development that children develop during play, particularly dramatic play, in their preschool years.

To a great extent, social development becomes a crucial factor in determining children's ability to be successful in school and life. Children who exhibit appropriate social development are able to make friends and interact positively with other children and adults. In family child care environments, where continuity of care is so important, young children can develop a sense of trust and security. Those are the very characteristics that allow them to develop necessary confidence. In smaller group settings, children are often less likely to feel lost and also less likely to go unnoticed than in large ones. Although challenging, the multiage group enrollment in an average family child care program can offer wonderful opportunities for social development in young children. Because children so readily learn from one another, older ones can significantly influence the positive social development of younger ones under the careful and watchful guidance of an involved provider.

Emotional and social development are intimately related when children's self-confidence and self-understanding take shape in early childhood. Social success depends in part on children's ability to express their feelings and to develop self-regulation and independence. Emotional maturity is reflected in their ability to balance happy and sad experiences. When developing a daily schedule of activities, it is important to include opportunities for children to feel independent and successful.

The smaller group size, range of ages and cultural backgrounds, and greater continuity of family child care should make it easier for you to support positive emotional development. When creating a daily schedule, it is helpful to see these elements of your program as strengths, not as liabilities, and to capitalize on these characteristics when developing activities. Children are more apt to feel capable and successful when they are recognized and given the opportunity to form attachments with you and the other children in the group.

Infant Social and Emotional Development

Attachment is an important issue to consider when introducing an infant to your child care environment. Attachment, which is sometimes referred to as bonding, is the connection that should occur between infants and their caregivers. For such connections to be beneficial, they need to be felt not only by the caregiver but also by the infants. For very young infants, providers often become "mother substitutes," which involves more than simply feeding and changing them. Fulfilling this role requires your willingness to nurture in a fashion similar to the way a mother would nurture a newborn. Infants who are not provided with appropriate nurturing are very often unable to form healthy attachments, which can impair their social and emotional development.

Because you very often have the opportunity to care for children from birth through preschool, you have the important opportunity to provide lasting bonds. Hold, touch, calm, rock, and make eye contact with each infant as often as possible every day. Remember, as infants form attachments, one attachment does not subtract from another. Assure new parents that infants maintain their first attachment to their parents while forming a connection with you or another adult. It is important for the parents and the provider to understand that the ability of infants to form many positive attachments is not only healthy and appropriate but will ultimately benefit them throughout life.

Attention to the daily routines and tasks that promote healthy social and emotional development in infants needs to begin the moment you know they are enrolling in your program. Communicate regularly with parents about this area of development. For infants to thrive, their child care setting needs to provide the type of nurturing care so frequently found in a healthy home with loving parents.

Infants Birth–6 months

One of the most dramatic examples of social and emotional development at this stage is an infant's ability to cry in order to get the attention of others. When caring for a group of children, it can be difficult to respond immediately to a crying infant. When you are caring for several infants, as well as older children, your immediate response may be almost impossible. It is important to remember, though, that crying is an essential form of infant communication. Often the manner in which you respond will determine an infant's ability to attach to you and feel secure in your child care setting.

During this stage of development, infants learn to recognize their primary caregivers. This includes not only their parents but you as well. Sometime between the ages of one to four months, an infant may reward you with a beautiful smile while you are changing her diaper. You may even be fortunate enough to have an infant in this age range laugh out loud when you interact with him. Capitalize on those special moments and reinforce them with your own smiles and laughter. Keep in mind that every interaction is an opportunity to reinforce positive social and emotional development.

Infants 6–12 months

During the end of the first year, infants very often begin to experience some anxiety when separated from their caregivers. This can occur when an infant is with you or with a parent. Both separation and stranger anxiety are common at this developmental stage. It is helpful to communicate to parents that such behavior is developmentally appropriate and that it reflects healthy social and emotional development. During this stage, it may be helpful to offer a daily routine that reinforces continuity. This allows infants to learn what to expect next while in your home and helps them adjust better to transition times, such as arrival and departure. As they feel more comfortable with your routine, they will generally be more trusting and less fearful in your child care setting. Although infants' fears seem very real and can produce anxiety, parents and providers who work together to establish consistent routines can help reinforce infants' confidence in their relationships.

Infants in this age group really begin to enjoy watching the other children in your program. At this stage they begin to realize that other children are different from you. Provide opportunities in which infants can closely yet safely observe the other children. This presents wonderful opportunities for their social development. Older children usually enjoy being given the opportunity to model various behaviors as well.

Activities or games that require you to be directly involved with infants, such as pat-a-cake are good ways to promote social and emotional growth. Your one-on-one interaction will produce positive results.

Infants 12–18 months

Infants in this age range are beginning to enjoy playing independently. They do not need to rely on you for constant stimulation. Although infants do not share or necessarily play with one another at this stage, they may, for example, play with blocks while other children are also playing with blocks. This type of play is called *parallel play*; it is more simultaneous than cooperative.

These infants may understand what "no" means but often choose to ignore it. Therefore, you will frequently need to intervene and in some instances physically remove those who resist direction. Your direct supervision during this period is very important, as is your ability to create a hazard-free environment. During this developmental stage, you cannot direct behavior from an adjacent room and expect older infants to automatically comply.

Stranger anxiety can be severe at this stage. Reassuring and consistent daily routines, as well as secure infant-provider attachment, can help to reduce the anxiety many infants experience during this period. The ability of a child to say no and the ability to differentiate between a familiar face and a stranger are important. As you attempt to reduce stranger anxiety, you need to be sensitive to each child's needs and background.

Toddler Social and Emotional Development

Toddlers should be learning how to wash their hands and faces, use the bathroom independently, and put on their own shoes. This is a special time, because you are supporting children while they develop independence. Remember to be a good role model, because a major part of the way toddlers learn is by watching and listening to the adults in their lives.

Toddlers show strong pride in their individual accomplishments. Your positive feedback about each success is very important. Acknowledge accomplishments and encourage toddlers to feel successful in their endeavors.

Toddlers can alternate between affection and anger in a moment's time. Your ability to quickly intervene is important. It is normal for toddlers to engage in parallel play. Be sure sufficient materials are available for parallel activities to prevent stress over the supply and demand of popular materials.

Older toddlers may begin to understand how their behavior affects the behavior of other children and adults. This can sometimes result in a toddler attempting to gain attention through inappropriate behavior. Your ability to respond appropriately helps toddlers begin to understand how their needs intersect with the needs of others. Demonstrate options, provide examples of positive behavior, and encourage problem solving to provide a great foundation for healthy social and emotional development.

Preschool-age Social and Emotional Development

Social and emotional development in three-year-olds blossoms when they engage in silly behavior and act funny in precocious ways. When three-year-olds have adults and peers as their audience, they never seem to run out of material. They are much more independent than they were at age two, and you will hear the words "I can do it myself" frequently. Three-year-olds, like toddlers, usually prefer to play alone or in parallel play and are often just beginning to interact with their peers. In considering this stage of development, you will need to ensure that your child care area is set up for all these types of play. Three-year-olds are beginning to understand the concepts of taking turns and sharing. They love to be recognized, and they are beginning to express feelings and emotions in appropriate ways. Healthy preschoolers are generally happy most of the time and are beginning to understand limits and rules.

As preschoolers age, they need many opportunities to explore, investigate, and talk about the world around them. They are beginning to rely less and less on adults, and they enjoy spending more time with other children in the child care setting. Preschoolers often appear fearless, but as they become more adept at telling the difference between reality and fantasy, they may cling to adults while working through these feelings. A good family child care program provides appropriate balance by offering many opportunities for independence while providing support, guidance, and protection.

Older preschoolers have an increased attention span. They are developing patience and friendships. Older preschoolers are also becoming more aware of sexuality. This is part of their natural curiosity about themselves and the world around them. Preschoolers are also beginning to use words because of the effect language has on adults and peers. Children at this stage want your attention, and they are regularly testing limits.

Social and Emotional Milestones

Infant Social and Emotional Development Milestones

Milestone	Generally Begins
Makes demanding cries	Birth–1 month
Shows sense of trust	Birth–1 month
Shows attachment (responds positively) to significant adults	Birth–1 month
Makes eye contact	Birth–1 month
Coos	1–3 months
Cries to demand attention	1–3 months
Smiles at the sound of familiar voices	1–3 months
Smiles at strangers	1–3 months
Tracks moving persons or objects	1–3 months
Babbles and laughs to get adult attention	3–6 months
Responds to smiles with smiling	3–6 months
Looks and listens for purpose	3–6 months
Pays close attention to older children and their actions	3–6 months
Calms self	3–6 months
Distinguishes voices of important, familiar people	6–9 months
Can distinguish voice tones and emotions	6–9 months
Plays games with adults and older children	6–9 months
Begins to feel anxiety on separation from familiar adults (separation anxiety)	9–12 months
Begins to feel anxiety in the presence of strangers (stranger anxiety)	9–12 months
Appears angry	9–12 months
Explores environment	9–12 months
May enjoy parallel play but does not play with peers; cannot yet share toys or possessions	12–18 months
Begins to imitate older siblings or peers	12–18 months
Shows signs of teasing adults	12–18 months

(Continued)

(Continued)

Milestone	Generally Begins
Understands the meaning of "no" but often resists directions and must be physically removed	14–18 months
Washes face and hands	16–24 months

Toddler Social and Emotional Development Milestones

Milestone	Generally Begins
Initiates separation from caregivers	18–24 months
Looks for "home base" or significant adult during difficult situations, for comfort and approval	18–24 months
Shows attachment to significant adults	18–24 months
Shows signs of stress when family members initiate separation	18–24 months
May enter strong negative stage, "no" to everything	18–24 months
Is toilet trained	18 months–3 years
Fear of strangers diminishes	2–2 ½ years
Shows strong pride in accomplishments, especially physical	2–2 ½ years
Shows independence in washing hands, dressing, and selecting clothing	2–2 ½ years
Is interested in anatomy	2–2 ½ years
Has tantrums	2–2 ½ years
Engages in parallel play	2–2 ½ years
Can identify and talk about personal feelings	2 ½–3 years
Can identify and talk about others' feelings	2 ½–3 years
Shows interest in helping	2 ½–3 years
Can recite rules but cannot follow them consistently	2 ½–3 years
Occasionally shows respect for other people and possessions	2 ½–3 years
Becomes greatly interested in the outside world	2 ½–3 years

Preschool-age Social and Emotional Development Milestones

Milestone	Generally Begins
Shows independence	3 years
Engages in solitary play	3 years
Begins to engage in associative play	3 years
Begins to show perspective	3 years
Begins taking turns	3 years
Begins to share	3 years
Begins to express feelings and emotions in appropriate manner	3 years
Enjoys helping with household tasks	3 years
Likes to be silly and make others laugh	3 years
Begins to understand some limits and rules	3 years
Begins to seek attention and approval	3 years
Makes simple choices (between two objects)	3 years
Engages in pretend play	3 years
Is becoming more responsible	4 years
Engages primarily in associative play	4 years
Has an increasing attention span	4 years
Is developing patience	4 years
Is developing friendships	4 years
Engages in group play	4 years
Role-plays	4 years
Plays simple games with rules	5 years
Follows and makes simple rules	5 years
Shows strong emotions	5 years
Often plays with peers	5 years
Is self-directed	5 years
Is sensitive to the feelings of others	5 years

Unit 5

Quality Care for Children

Providing materials and equipment that enhance learning opportunities for children of all ages is critical to a good child care environment. Open, uncluttered space is also important. A developmentally appropriate learning environment should provide materials that support fine- and gross-motor skill development, cognitive development, and communication and language development, along with social and emotional development.

It is extremely important that the materials and equipment used in your child care setting are safe. Make sure that anything a child uses, including cribs or playpens, are appropriate for the weight and mobility of children. Check recall lists regularly for unsafe toys and equipment. Always read labels and instructions carefully. Because family child care includes multiage groups, it is not uncommon for younger children to want to play with and do everything the older children do. Use age-appropriate equipment.

Your ability to directly supervise is extremely important. As anyone who has provided care for a young child knows, it's amazing what can happen in the blink of an eye. Once mobile, children are astonishing in their speed. Direct supervision helps you to be close enough to intervene quickly when necessary. For example, it is normal for toddlers to have trouble playing well with other children, and behaviors such as biting are common. Consequently, your supervision and guidance are needed to support positive behavior and protect all the children in your care.

Young children want to do things. Their need to achieve and accomplish is intuitive. Children develop independence and feel competent if their physical and mental health are provided for in a supportive environment. Your primary role is to provide that supportive environment.

Supporting Children

Whether all children develop independence and a sense of competence depends to a great extent on how their work is valued by the people they love and respect.

- Let children know you are glad to be their child care provider. Give them personal attention and encouragement. Do fun things together.
- Set good examples by always saying "please" and "thank you."
- Help children find ways to solve conflicts with other children.
- Be affectionate.
- Show children how to include everyone in their games.
- Thank children when they do kind things for one another.

Children need to feel successful in their endeavors. In a quality family child care environment, fostering a sense of competence is important. How does a provider do this? An effective program should help children to feel successful as a normal part of their daily routine. For example, providers need to include child-sized furniture and equipment whenever possible, not because it is cute, but because it helps children do things without adult assistance. Materials need to be accessible so children can feel more independent and consequently less dependent on you. Providing child-sized containers for milk or juice, which preschool children can use to pour their own drinks at the lunch table, is an example of a simple way to enhance independence.

Equipment Safety and Placement

In planning how to arrange your child care space, you need to provide opportunities for appropriate physical development. The ability to run, for example, is an important developmental benchmark. Unfortunately, in some child care settings, when children run indoors, doing so results in a time-out. Whether you provide care in an apartment or a house, it is your responsibility to incorporate activities that enhance the total development of children—and that includes space for them.

Arrange your child care space to accommodate the routines of sleeping, eating, safe physical movement, and diapering and toilet training. Every family child care setting is unique; nonetheless, you must consider some basic elements of what children need when planning and designing or evaluating your current space:

- soft and cozy areas in the indoor and outdoor environments
- open areas with a variety of surfaces to explore
- low furniture for exploration and balance support
- safe materials and equipment

Balance the hardness in a room with soft objects such as beanbag chairs and large floor pillows. If possible, establish a spot to keep unfinished projects and artwork. Try to establish personal storage space for each child. If your house has small rooms, designate each of your licensed rooms for certain activities. For example, your kitchen could be used for art projects and table games, while the family room could be used for dramatic play and group time. It's a good idea to make popular areas like the dramatic play area as large as possible.

 ## SAFETY NOTE
Ensuring a Safe Environment

You must ensure that all the equipment you use is safe. Some of your equipment may have been donated or purchased at yard sales or used furniture stores. Always be aware of what you are buying or what is being donated to your program. You should review recall lists frequently. Check to ensure that equipment has all the necessary screws and bolts and that everything is appropriately secured. Check for cracked or broken wood. Be aware of lead-based paint; if you are using painted furniture or equipment, make sure the painted surface is lead free. Always read labels and instructions carefully. When you are creating your learning areas, remember that open floor space is important for healthy child development. Avoid clutter and the temptation to include too many toys or pieces of equipment. Look for creative storage opportunities and review the following information:

Physical Environment

- Safety locks or latches must be installed and fully functional on all drawers and cabinets where hazardous materials are stored.
- Gates or doors that block stairways and/or rooms containing inappropriate items should be in place at all times when young children are in care.
- All accessible electrical outlets should have safety covers in place.

- All mats or rugs at exits should be skid proof.
- Electrical cords must be kept out of toddlers' reach and out of doorways and traffic paths.
- All storage units must be stable and secured against sliding, collapsing, or tipping.
- No disease-bearing animals, such as turtles or parrots, should be allowed in the child care area.
- Stairs and stairways must be kept free of boxes, toys, and other clutter.
- Trash should be kept covered and stored away from where food is prepared or stored.
- No-pest strips or other products that kill insects or vermin can be used where children are present.

Materials and Equipment

- Toys and play equipment should be checked often for sharp edges, small parts, sharp points, and potential choking hazards.
- No hinged toy boxes should be used.
- Televisions and all other media equipment must be secured appropriately to prevent tipping.
- Curtains, pillows, blankets, and cloth toys should be made of flame-resistant materials and laundered regularly.
- Stable step stools are available when needed.
- All equipment used by children must be in good repair and free of splinters and sharp edges.

Your Role When Caring for Infants

The wonderful things that usually define home-based care—small group size, multiple ages of enrolled children, and a home environment—work well in providing care for infants. Including infants in a family child care program has the potential to contribute to the overall healthy development of all the enrolled children. Rather than confining infants to an infant room, family child care providers can supervise interactions among all the children, greatly contributing to a positive early learning experience for everyone.

Infants in family child care often spend more waking hours with their child care providers than with almost any other adults, including family members. Therefore, it is very important to be aware of the developmental needs of infants. Your infant curriculum should address all the developmental learning domains: physical and motor, cognitive, communication and language, and social and emotional. When scheduling daily activities that promote skill development, you should not ignore the needs of infants.

Occasionally infants are placed in swings or infant seats for extended periods of time, thus excluding them from many of the program's daily activities. When questioned about this, providers sometimes say the infants are contained for safety reasons or that they need their rest and should not be disturbed. In other cases, providers may feel that including infants in an activity is simply too labor intensive and cannot be accomplished in the family child care setting. In reality, it is often a matter of a provider not fully understanding the developmental needs of infants.

Before accepting an infant into your program, you should determine how you will include this child in a manner that will benefit all of the enrolled children, including the infant. Look at your available space. Does your setting allow you to provide for an infant's appropriate physical development? Is there sufficient space for infants to have tummy time, during which they can begin to crawl and stretch; space that is protected and accessible? Does your setting provide ample opportunities for infants to engage in activities that will promote communication and language skills, as well as cognitive, social, and emotional development? Do you fully understand what an infant needs in order to grow and develop and how you can provide all of the necessary developmental opportunities in your family child care program? This unit is designed to assist you in addressing these questions.

To accommodate infants' developmental needs while still addressing the needs of other children, you must capitalize on the times when you can devote your full attention to the infant(s) in your care. Recognize that much of what you do naturally constitutes a large part of your infant curriculum. In this unit, you will find information that clarifies your role in providing care for infants, as well as tips that will help you create an appropriate infant area. Note that the information about infant development and activities is divided into three age groups. This accommodates the broad developmental differences between a newborn and a one-and-a-half-year-old.

You take on special responsibilities when caring for infants. The way you touch, talk to, and nurture them can have a lasting effect on their future development. The bonding that takes place between you is necessary so they can progress in all areas of development.

When there are infants in a family child care setting, there must be an area where the equipment and toys are designated specifically for them and where appropriate safety precautions are in place. This does not mean that infants should be confined to that area exclusively. It means that there are times in the day, such as naptime, when infants need an area where they can sleep without much disturbance. Infants also need time and space to safely use age-appropriate equipment and materials, such as toys. There should be adequate space, and equipment should be arranged to accommodate sleeping, eating, safe physical movement, and diapering. The setting should also include these elements:

- soft and cozy areas in the indoor and outdoor environment
- open areas with a variety of surfaces to explore
- low furniture so that older infants can explore and pull themselves up
- a daily schedule of activities that includes infants

Every family child care setting is unique. The following are some basic things every program should consider when planning and designing an infant area.

Materials for Infants

Infants' play should be full of exploration and discovery. Infants should be encouraged to use all their senses to examine the color, shape, texture, and movement of objects. They need the opportunity to shake things for sound, push things for movement, and place safe objects in their mouths for taste and touch. You should choose toys that stimulate their senses and allow for active involvement. It is helpful to have a place to store toys and equipment designated for your infants. Keep in mind that you want to foster independence rather than dependence. As infants become more mobile, allow them access to your storage area so they can locate toys safely, as well as have the opportunity to learn to clean up.

Many appropriate playthings for infants can be found in your home or can be easily made. Remember: anything a provider gives an infant to play with should be checked out first for safety. Objects like large plastic hair rollers or a wooden spoon with a face drawn on the bowl will delight infants. As you know, each child is different. What may be a delightful toy for one child can become a weapon for another. Don't only check out each object for safety—closely observe how children are using it in the course of their play.

 **SAFETY NOTE**

Direct Supervision

There is no legitimate substitute for direct supervision. Although something may not appear to be hazardous, it is important for you to observe the infants' play and to intervene immediately if one of them is in distress.

Infants need play materials that stimulate their senses and allow them to acquire necessary skills through play. The following is a list of inexpensive play materials you can make. Please remember that anything you create for infants should be checked carefully for wear and tear and possible choking hazards. These play materials include all types of textures to provide sensory stimulation for infants. This list includes materials that are soft, smooth, rough, bumpy, and fuzzy:

- Make a cloth ball by stuffing an old towel or scrap fabric with nylon stockings and sewing it into a round shape.
- Make cloth dolls or animals from old towels or material scraps stuffed with old, clean socks or other cotton or wool fibers.
- Remove the labels from an empty juice can and ensure all edges are smooth. The can is something smooth to play with and roll around.
- Tie some netting together to form a puffball, and watch the infant experiment while playing with this "prickly" toy.
- Make a crib mobile or busy box that can be attached to the crib and may include securely attached infant-friendly activities and materials. Some busy boxes may include brightly colored beads as well as mirrors and/or buttons and levers to manipulate. A busy box should not be a substitute for caregiver interaction.

Infants also like to play with these items:

- washable, cuddly toys and stuffed animals for awake time (these items are not recommended for sleeping infants because of possible suffocation)
- sturdy wooden or durable plastic rattles
- plastic key rings
- nonbreakable plastic mirror

- teething rings and other teething toys
- grasping toys, such as rubber rings and toys with handles made of pliable, nontoxic material
- toy telephones
- balls of different sizes and textures
- fill-and-dump toys, such as cups, spoons, and pails
- large plastic or wooden animals
- soft cloth blocks
- cloth dolls and animals
- stacking and nesting toys
- books made from cloth, heavy cardboard, or nontoxic plastic
- plastic measuring cups
- measuring spoons on a secure ring
- wooden spoons
- boxes with lids, such as shoe boxes
- old-fashioned wooden clothespins
- pots, pans, and lids
- empty bandage tins
- baskets and bins
- large plastic napkin rings

SAFETY NOTE
Ensuring Safe Spaces for Infants

Cribs and Changing Tables

- Crib mattresses should fit snugly.
- Crib slats should not be more than 2⅜ inches apart.
- Cribs should be assembled properly. There should not be any missing screws or bolts.
- Cribs and any other baby furniture should not be painted with lead-based paints.
- Cribs and playpens should not be placed near windows.
- A carpet or rug that would soften the impact if an infant were to fall should be placed beneath all cribs and changing tables.
- All changing tables should have safety belts, which should be used whenever an infant is on the changing table.

- All changing supplies should be out of an infant's reach but within reach of the provider.

Hanging Items

- Drapery cords and/or blind cords should be well out of reach of children and away from cribs.
- All crib gyms, hanging toys, and decorations should be removed from a crib as soon as an infant can rise up on his hands and knees.

Toys

- All toys and other items should be larger than 1¾ inches in diameter. Choke testers can be purchased to determine appropriate diameter if you are in doubt.
- Toy parts or pieces of toys should not be allowed in the napping area.

Play Spaces

- Areas where infants crawl should be clean and hazard free at all times.
- Mats or quilts should be available for infants who are just beginning to roll over or are having tummy time.
- Low furniture should be arranged so that infants can pull themselves up or use it as a support when walking.
- Play areas should be sufficiently protected so that the normal play of older children will not endanger crawling infants.
- No lights should be placed near or touching drapes, blankets, or bedspreads. Never place towels or other fabric over a lamp to reduce the light in a room.

Your Role When Caring for Toddlers

Toddlers—fabulous, fabulous, toddlers! It's nearly impossible to feel depressed or sad for very long in the company of toddlers. Their enthusiasm and exuberance are contagious. Between eighteen and thirty-six months, a great amount of development occurs. Young children who only a few months ago were seemingly almost totally reliant upon you are now becoming more and more independent. Toddlers are generally able to run independently, eat with utensils, and identify body parts. Many toddlers have developed both the coordination necessary to kick a ball forward and the ability to communicate their wishes and intentions. Toddlers are more communicative, and when willing, are usually better able to concentrate for longer periods of time. Many providers favor this stage of development because it allows for more feedback from the children about the types of activities to include when developing daily schedules for them. Although toddlers require a consistent routine, their needs usually require less structure than those of infants.

In addition, there is the pleasure that comes from watching emerging personalities and the satisfaction that occurs from seeing the progress children have made in response to the support and stimulation provided in your program. If you began caring for children as infants, it is especially gratifying to see them progress and thrive.

For many providers, the characteristics that define this stage of development create unique challenges. Toddlers often exhibit behaviors such as biting, short attention spans, and the seeming inability or unwillingness to follow directions. In family child care programs, where staff is usually limited to one provider, or a provider and one approved assistant, these behaviors can produce a variety of challenges, so it is important to understand what is developmentally appropriate for children in this age group. Activities that are well planned and age appropriate for toddlers will go a long way in assisting you during your child care day. It is also important to understand how to guide good behavior.

When you understand how toddlers develop and grow, you are better able to create a child-friendly environment that supports this development. This includes keeping materials that you do not want them to investigate inaccessible. Understanding rules is an important developmental benchmark for toddlers. Create simple rules and include activities that are age appropriate for the developmental stages of all the children in your program. The following materials are grouped by developmental domain:

Physical and Motor Development

- Manipulative toys, such as connecting blocks, assist with small-muscle development as well as eye-hand coordination.
- Large equipment, including tricycles, big wheels, balls, boxes, and hollow blocks, allows toddlers to use their whole bodies.
- Brooms, sponges, shovels, and buckets are tools children can use to accomplish tasks.

- Buttoning buttons, zipping zippers, and independent feeding promote fine-motor skill development.
- Turning the pages of a book enhances fine-motor skill development.
- Providing sufficient and accessible space for jumping and running (as well as equipment and games) encourages the development of coordination.

Cognitive Development

- Manipulative toys, such as puzzles, peg-boards, and connecting pieces (always be aware of choking hazards), help children understand trial and error. Eating and dressing can also provide practice in this area.
- Filling and emptying objects, stacking, then knocking down cups or blocks, hammering and pounding, and opening and closing provide toddlers opportunities to explore cause and effect.
- Different types of fruits and vegetables, different-sized spoons, and colored socks in a laundry basket teach toddlers how to sort and classify objects.
- Exploring materials, such as water and sand, playdough, paint and shaving cream, different types of cloth, and different fruits and vegetables, allows toddlers to examine the sensory details of each item.
- Engaging in arts and crafts encourages toddlers' creativity and small-motor development. Remember to supervise closely.
- Examining and exploring age-appropriate nature items are cost-effective ways to introduce object recognition and memory retention.

Communication and Language Development

- Include regular periods for storytelling and reading, and have an accessible supply of books that children can look at independently. Read poems aloud so children can learn about rhythm and repeated sounds in language. Have a comfortable area for looking at books. Read more about the importance of reading with children on page 195.
- Help toddlers identify the words for familiar objects, such as the figures in a dollhouse, parts of the body, and so on. Create activities and games that build children's object identification and memory retention skills.

- Create as many opportunities as possible for learning and listening to age-appropriate songs and for playing instruments. Music can also provide a beneficial backdrop to a family child care environment. Some children in family child care programs can identify the time of day and its associated activity based on the music played to them.

Social and Emotional Development

- Provide duplicate toys and equipment for toddlers, as toddlers should not be expected to share. Duplicate toys and supplies encourage parallel play that eventually leads toddlers to cooperative play with others.
- Always rotate supplies and toys to avoid boredom. Provide as many materials as possible that toddlers can use on their own without adult assistance.
- Offer puppets and props so toddlers can pretend to be the important adults in their lives.
- Encourage dramatic play that allows toddlers to act out various roles, especially those roles usually limited to adults. Dramatic play allows toddlers to experience success in areas not ordinarily available to them, such as working in a store or car wash. Change the dramatic play area frequently. Set up a post office for three or four weeks, then try a garage, store, or restaurant for a few weeks.
- Create at least one private space where a toddler can get away from the other children but can still be seen by you. An example of this might be a large painted household appliance box with pillows inside.

Your Role When Caring for Preschool Children

A good family and home setting provides a preschool child with extraordinary opportunities for learning and growth. Through daily care and concern, parents know exactly how to respond to their young children in most situations. They know when to intervene with encouragement and protection, and when to back off and allow their children the opportunity to test their capacities and develop new skills. Good parents know when to shield their children from sadness and worries and when to give them the opportunity to deal with anxieties.

The kinds of daily interaction that take place between parents and young children from three to six years of age are not the types of interactions that are always easily understood by someone outside of the family. Sometimes it is difficult to understand how preschool children think and feel about their family members. Yet how a preschool child acts at home and what the child needs from home are important when thinking about quality family child care. You should always reflect on whether the children in your program are receiving the kind of love, care, attention, and stimulation they would receive in a healthy home while they are in your care.

Development in one domain cannot really be understood without considering the child's development in each of the others. In creating your schedule of activities, be sure that all developmental domains are addressed. To do this effectively, you must understand each child's competencies as well as the next milestone associated with each competency.

As you review the developmental stages, you will find it necessary to reflect on your daily schedule of activities, identifying the activities that support the children and help them grow and learn. If you find that your daily schedule is not accommodating these, then now is the time to make constructive changes. Use this curriculum as a resource to help you incorporate materials and activities that create a meaningful and effective schedule.

There is no question that one of the biggest challenges in family child care is the issue of available space. In recognizing that you are caring for children of mixed ages in your home, this curriculum reflects your need to designate areas for different ages and activities. When you create activity areas, you also create learning areas. Those two concepts should be interchangeable. Learning areas should allow preschoolers to make choices, encourage active learning, and offer hands-on experiences. Your learning areas should also foster social skills through interactive cooperation, communication as children talk freely, and space for movement.

When you are thinking about creating preschool learning areas in your home, it is helpful to list the types of learning activities that should occur as part of your preschool curriculum:

- language arts
- math
- science
- art
- music
- small-motor

- large-motor
- dramatic
- blocks
- outdoor play area
- quiet place

Examine your available space carefully. Your kitchen table can be the learning area for many learning experiences. If you have limited space, you can certainly use one area of a room interchangeably. For example, a corner that is used for blocks in the morning may be used for dramatic play in the afternoon. If you make signs to identify the learning activity and change them when applicable, they will assist the children in identifying specific areas.

In home-based care, you usually have the advantage of multiple rooms. Many educators believe there is an advantage to not having large open spaces in which children are prone to run. Organize your areas so that like toys are together. For example, puzzles, sewing cards, and manipulatives should be together; writing materials grouped; art supplies grouped. Separate the noisy areas from the quiet ones. The more physical activities, such as dramatics and block play, should be in one part of a room, while books and manipulatives can be in another part of the room.

You may have bedrooms or a den that you can use for specific learning areas. You may want to store materials in containers with wheels or casters for easy storage or in closets or cupboards so that at the end of your child care day, you can easily return the room to its domestic purpose. Remember: your ability to supervise at all times is important. Look at each preschool learning area in terms of function as well as your ability to see and hear the children. What follows are basic materials for preschool learning:

For Physical Development

Large-motor development provides for physical fitness, coordination and strength of large muscles, and release of feelings and frustrations in preschool children. The following is a list of materials to be considered when creating your preschool area. Some of these materials may be available at your local playground. In creating effective learning areas, you should look at resources outside of your home as well as at what you have inside. Suggested materials include:

- balls
- balance beam
- bean bags
- age-appropriate climbing equipment
- hula hoops
- tumbling mats
- slide
- music source
- jump ropes
- balloons
- riding toys

Small-motor skill development for preschoolers is equally important. Your small-motor area will assist children in increasing attention span, developing eye-hand coordination and small muscle control, while learning the concepts of size, shape, color, and pattern. Suggested materials include:

- puzzles
- puzzle rack
- beads
- sewing cards
- lacing activities
- peg-board
- Etch A Sketch
- dressing toys
- stacking toys
- locks and keys
- nuts and bolts
- take-apart toys
- scissors
- hole punch
- clay
- playdough

- pattern cards
- snap toys
- paper and pencils

For Cognitive Development

Two areas of learning that enhance cognitive development for preschoolers are math and science. Creating areas where these types of activities can occur both with your assistance and independently will greatly enrich your preschool curriculum.

Through exposure to math, your preschool children learn counting, grouping, comparisons, patterns, time, money measurement, addition, subtraction, geometric shapes, and problem solving. Suggested materials include:

- toy clock
- pennies
- play money
- rulers
- balance scale
- flannel board
- objects to count (shells, rocks, buttons, etc.)
- popsicle sticks
- toys
- geometric shapes
- tactile numerals
- puzzles
- measuring cups and spoons
- dominoes
- paper, pencils
- chalkboard
- computer

Through science, preschool children learn to experiment, solve problems, make decisions, develop concepts about science and nature, and develop sensory skills. Suggested materials include:

- magnifying glass
- magnets

- plants
- prisms
- balance scale
- exhibits (nature collections of rocks, shells, insects, etc.)
- science books, magazines
- pictures and posters
- digital thermometer
- feely box
- terrarium
- seeds, nuts, leaves, flowers
- bird nests, feathers

For Communication and Language Development

The language learning area for your preschoolers should foster oral language, listening skills, vocabulary, letter recognition, rhymes, phonics, reading-readiness skills, social skills, sight vocabulary, writing skills, and a positive attitude about reading. Suggested materials include:

- books
- magnetic letters
- tactile letters
- letter puzzles
- picture file
- puppets
- flannelboard
- reading-readiness games
- alphabet bingo
- lotto
- match-up games
- same-and-different games
- typewriter
- rebus pictures
- chalkboard
- paper and pencils

- blank books
- sequence cards
- wipe-off cards
- tape recorder

For Social and Emotional Development

Art areas promote creative expression in young children. They also enhance imagination and cooperation skills. Suggested materials include:

- brushes
- paints
- fingerpaints
- crayons
- chalk
- markers
- paper
- tissue paper
- glue
- recycled materials
- clay
- playdough
- scissors
- stapler
- tape
- cotton
- magazines
- wallpaper books
- paper clips
- craft sticks

A dramatic play area can greatly enhance preschool children's ability to learn cooperative play and social skills. It also allows them to express creativity. Suggested materials include:

- large empty boxes
- old jewelry

- telephone (both old handsets and cellular phones are interesting to children)
- empty, clean food boxes and containers
- baby carriage
- doll bed
- puppets
- stuffed animals
- dolls and doll clothes (make your collection diverse in race and gender)
- child-sized table and chairs
- secure full-length mirror
- purses, shoes, hats, ties
- kitchen equipment, including stove, refrigerator, pots, pans, dishes, toy broom, sweeper
- child-sized ironing board and iron
- dress-up clothes (all types)
- playsilks

Nurturing Children's Learning

Children learn in a positive environment. Creating an environment where "no" and "Don't touch" are replaced by "yes" and "Let's see how this works" fosters positive learning. Remember that items that are not appropriate for young children to explore should not be accessible.

Children learn through the quality of your care. Children who are not fed properly or who are tired or stressed have more difficulty benefiting from learning experiences. The quality of your care is reflected in a well-balanced daily schedule of activities that meets the physical and emotional needs of children in your program.

Children learn through experimentation. Activities need to include opportunities to try, touch, see, hear, smell, and do new things. Young children need opportunities to try and fail and try again. The safety of the child care environment and the trust established between you and each child should consistently reinforce experimentation and exploration.

Young children learn by moving. They sometimes appear to be in perpetual motion. Often their attention span for some activities is limited. Usually, if they are allowed to move about and engage in whole body experiences, they will use their hands, feet, head, and body to learn. Don't complain about their energy—find inventive ways to capitalize on it.

Children learn through their senses. Incorporate activities that allow young children the opportunity to use all their senses: seeing, hearing, touching, tasting, and smelling. Cooking and gardening are wonderful activities to stimulate all senses.

Children learn by doing. Teaching in family child care often involves incorporating a few age-appropriate chores. Many young children love to sweep with brooms or mops. Wiping a table can be a great activity for a toddler, since it does not require a lot of verbal instruction.

Young children learn through play. You need to acknowledge the value of supervised play while you develop your daily schedule. Play is what young children do best and enjoy most. In fostering total development, play is children's work. Incorporating creative types of play and games offers children many different learning experiences.

Children learn through language. Giving them words is most probably one of the greatest gifts you can give. Children need to be able to verbalize their experiences and feelings. Reading, talking, listening, and singing are important elements of your curriculum.

Children learn through imitation. They imitate others constantly. In a family child care environment, children will alternate between imitating children older and younger than themselves. You are constantly on stage, for children will often mirror your language and your behavior.

Children learn through repetition. They build knowledge based on repetition and accumulated experience. This is why young children can patiently listen to the same story for what seems like hundreds of times. Patience and a willingness to repeat favorite activities over and over are a necessary part of any successful toddler curriculum.

Children learn through exposure. It is often said that young children are like sponges. If that statement is true, it is important to believe that the more exposure to positive stimulus in a safe and protected setting, the more they will learn. The more positive and varied the experiences, the better!

Nurturing Children's Growth

The more a child is cuddled, snuggled, and held, the more secure and independent that child will become. Young children, especially infants, need to be held often for bonding and normal brain development to occur. Be sure to allow sufficient time in the day to snuggle and hold infants. While holding an infant in your arms, walk or rock the child back and forth while talking softly to him. With older children, snuggle while reading a book, hold hands while going for a walk, and give hugs when they are needed.

Young children respond to verbal cues. Verbal cues can include the sounds adults often use when talking with young children. Infants may respond to soft cooing sounds or higher pitched inflections. As you come to know each child in your care, you will be able to adapt your pitch and emphasis based on the child's response. Don't be afraid to experiment. When you communicate with young children, you should encourage vocal response. For example, imitate the sound an infant makes, and encourage the infant to respond to your sounds. Give a toddler the words to say, "I'm angry that you took my toy." These types of interactions assist in the development of language skills. Daily routines offer some of the best opportunities for interacting verbally with infants. For example, talk to them while changing their diapers, feeding them, and cleaning them up afterward. Talk to them while preparing lunch or supervising activities involving other children. The more you communicate and encourage responses, the more opportunities for language and communication development occur.

Young children also possess a natural response to music, in part because of their conditioning in the womb to rhythm, sound, and movement. Even very small infants may be soothed by music. A good choice of music is soft instrumental music or lullabies. Repetitious melodies, such as "Rock-a-Bye Baby" or "Row, Row, Row Your Boat" are generally well received by most infants and toddlers. Preschool-age children are ready for more complicated rhythms.

Activities that encourage young children to use their sense of sight and to enhance visual development are important. Invite infants to track an object. Toddlers and preschoolers enjoy playing I Spy. You may find the child turning away if the routine or game has become too familiar. As in all activities, it is important to be attentive to changes in temperaments and patterns of behavior. Not every child will respond or engage in the same manner.

The Importance of a Daily Schedule

Along with your nurturing and positive attention to a safe environment and healthy growth and development, you should provide children of all ages with opportunities for positive interaction with other children. As you plan your daily schedule, capitalize on your multiage enrollment. Make sure there is plenty of time each day when even the infants are able to observe and interact with children of all ages. Even the smallest infants can benefit from opportunities to hear and see the activity around them. Infants' cognitive and emotional growth is tied to early experiences. Because you are in a position to provide opportunities for many of those rich early learning experiences in your family child care setting, the importance of your role cannot be overstated.

Learning in child care involves just about every interaction that occurs between an adult and a child. You constantly demonstrate appropriate behaviors through your tone of voice, smiles, acts of kindness, and tender touches—all are important parts of the early learning experience. Your schedule of activities should include sufficient time for these types of interactions as well as more structured learning activities. A successful daily schedule is balanced between routine care and teaching, inclusive of all the developmental domains, and reflective of the different ways children learn.

When you are planning a family child care schedule, a daily routine that works well for you and the participating children is a must. As a family child care provider, you are a time manager. Many of you do not have additional staff. You do it all. Not only do you wipe tears, bottoms, and noses, but you must also assure a safe and sanitary environment at all times. You not only prepare food, you clean up as well. To successfully deal with all of these tasks, you need to establish a daily routine that allows you and the children to have consistent expectations about what will occur during the course of the day. Each day should consistently include a variety of learning activities:

- active (dancing, digging)
- quiet (reading, puzzles)
- group (singing, listening to stories)
- independent (building, pretending)
- free choice (children choose)
- structured (provider directs)
- indoor (art, sensory)
- outdoor (climbing, art)
- transition times (arrival, toileting)
- eating (snacks, meals)
- naps (sleep, quiet rest time)

A daily routine needs structure but should not be rigid. It is important to be able to make changes when necessary. An unexpected stormy day means the walk to the corner store may have to wait. A day when one or more of the children are coping with colds may also be a good reason to change planned activities.

Create a routine by assigning blocks of time that correspond to the activities and tasks you and the children repeat each day. These repeated activities include the children's arrival, cleanup, hand washing, lunch, outdoor time, and naps or rest time. Time should also be allotted for each day's new activities while keeping in mind what can realistically be accomplished. Very simply, in managing your program, it is important that you create a routine you can live with. An experienced provider once said that the secret of her success was that she understood that not only do children require a quiet moment but so do most providers. Once she knew this, things began to come together. She was able to develop a daily routine that reflected her philosophy to support the children without forgetting her own needs.

This curriculum offers four sample daily schedules. Sometimes what looks good on paper does not correspond with the reality of your environment or your enrollment. Don't be afraid to change or alter a daily routine that doesn't work well in your program. Just make sure the children understand the changes and are not surprised by them.

When establishing a successful daily routine, you should consider how children grow and develop. Your philosophy can best be described as how you might explain the uniqueness of your program to a prospective parent. What are the characteristics of your program that set it apart from other child care programs? What is your style with young children? What do you believe are your best practices for providing healthy growth and development?

The provider who shared her secret of success had determined that the pace of her daily routine needed to reflect the fact that she and the children benefited from unstructured quiet time. As a result, her daily routine offered a relaxed approach with an emphasis on the quality of activities rather than the quantity. She and the children were relaxed and happy. Establishing your philosophy makes it easier to develop a daily routine. Your priorities will help you plan daily activities that support the overall goals of your program.

Identifying the abilities and needs of each child and then choosing activities to meet those abilities and needs constitute a seemingly simple formula for success. However, meeting the individual needs of each child through activities that are also appropriate for all the ages and stages of the children in your care can be challenging. Consequently, it's important to periodically examine your daily routine, as well as the specific activities included in those routines. A periodic assessment is necessary to determine whether the individual needs of children are successfully met. For example, how can you appropriately accommodate the developmental needs of Maria, who is about to take her first step, at the same time that you are accommodating the developmental needs of Mathew, who will begin kindergarten in the fall?

There are many homes where the family child care provider has either attempted to create a one-size-fits-all curriculum or has simply ignored the developmental needs of one age group to focus on another. Neither method is an effective choice for supporting all children. Many providers, even in programs where the children are all close in age, find that each child's interests and developmental needs can fall into a fairly broad range. Just as each family child care program is different, so each child is different. It is possible for a good daily schedule with a thoughtful selection of activities to be developed while accommodating each child. In order to do this, you must keep in mind that learning opportunities do not take place only while reading a book or creating an art project.

The type of learning that occurs during lunch, for example, is as important as any other learning experience. You can capitalize on that daily activity and incorporate all of your curriculum objectives. Think about what occurs when a child sits at a table with other children and successfully eats a pleasant meal. There is the opportunity for physical development as a result of eating good food, using appropriate utensils, and drinking from a cup. There is the opportunity for language development as a result of the conversation that should occur during the meal. There is the opportunity for social development as a result of positive interaction with peers and adults. There is the opportunity for emotional development as a result of the satisfaction gained from setting the table or assisting another child. There is the opportunity for cognitive development in identifying colors on the table, counting crackers, and discussing the origin of foods. The real secret to creating a successful daily schedule is to look closely at all the elements of your day and make each of them as meaningful as possible.

Partnering with Families

It would be a mistake to minimize the importance of children's parents or guardians on their education. Parents are children's first and most important teachers. Family child care providers need to demonstrate respect for the parents of children in their program. The more involved families are, the more academic success children will have in school. That also holds true with the learning and development that should occur in early child care settings. It is important to let parents know how much you value their children. Develop creative ways to keep communication open. In creating a child care environment that enhances the development and well-being of children, you and the parents need to work together.

A very real part of your responsibility is communicating any concerns you may have to parents, based on your observations, of the growth and development of their children. This is not always easy. Your preparation and your professionalism are very important.

Scheduling face-to-face meetings is preferable to attempting to communicate your concerns over the phone or by letter or e-mail. Be friendly and start off with positive comments. Keep your conversation focused on the child. Be prepared by having documented observations that reflect your concerns. Listen to what the parent has to say and try to remember that being defensive or argumentative is not in the best interest of the child. If there is a problem, brainstorm solutions and assist the parent to develop an action plan when applicable.

It is important to remember that your role as a provider requires you to share your observations, but you should not be diagnosing children based on past child care experiences you may have had. Each child is different. Sharing developmental milestone information with parents can be very helpful. Many communities have early intervention resources that can be of great assistance to both you and parents. Let parents know about any resources you are aware of in your community. Be supportive. Keep in mind that working together can only further enhance the well-being of their child.

Many providers have observed that some parents are more difficult to deal with than their children. Occasionally you may feel that parents are simply not interested in the quality of your care and are more focused on what you are charging and how late you will stay open to accommodate their child care needs. This can be frustrating. However, in establishing positive early learning goals for your program, you will need to find effective ways to communicate with all of the parents, including those who are challenging.

Some suggestions:

- Progress reports. The very name makes parents smile. Concerned parents want to know their child is progressing in a positive way. Use your developmental milestone chart and incorporate information that's applicable in your progress report. Many providers send this type of report home on a monthly basis. It is usually not difficult to identify something new that has occurred during the month as you watch the children grow and develop. This will also give you an opportunity to bring to the attention of parents your observations on any developmental delays that you may become aware of as you review the milestone information.

- Monthly or bimonthly meetings. Although you may see parents daily at drop-off and pickup time, there is generally little time to engage in much conversation. Those times of day are commonly the most hectic in a typical family child care environment. Parents are often anxious to get to work or home and do not want to chat. You are also usually very busy during those periods as well. You may also have parents who do not do the drop-off and pickup themselves but depend on other modes of transport, such as buses or extended family members. Scheduling face-to-face meetings at a convenient time for both you and a child's parents can provide for better working relationships and better provider-parent communication. Be prepared. Know what you want to say before the meeting begins. If there is paperwork you need or questions to which you need answers, let parents know before the meeting. Be conscious of time and try to keep things as on point as possible.

- Other options. Some providers hold potluck suppers for all of their parents. Others host arts and craft nights for families. Some providers invite parents to come at story time and read to the children. Other providers have created checklists that they send home each day with each child.

Whatever you choose to do to maximize the communication between you and the parents of children in your program, it can only enhance your ability to meet the individual needs of all the children.

The following are ideas you can implement to help parents feel secure and motivated to work with you to provide the best possible early learning experience.

- Schedule a pre-enrollment meeting at a time when you are not providing child care. Arrange to talk with parents at a place in your home where they can feel comfortable and your conversation will not be interrupted. Be friendly and relaxed. Actively listen to what parents have to say. Give them the opportunity to clearly state their child care needs. Be prepared to refer a family to another resource if you feel you cannot adequately meet the needs of both the parents and the child.

- Be straightforward about your licensing history. Parents of infants very often check with the licensing authority prior to interviewing a provider. If you have had licensing complaints or issues, it is much better for prospective parents to hear what occurred and how it was resolved from you.

- Provide prospective parents with a handbook that contains your policies. Parents of infants usually want easy access to their children. In many states, automatic access is a regulatory requirement. What is your policy? What are your expectations regarding naptime visits? Who supplies formula and diapering materials—you or the parent? What is your policy regarding breast-feeding? Does your setting comfortably accommodate breast-feeding? What is your policy regarding cloth diapering? What are your sick policies? When do you require a parent to leave work or school to pick up a sick child? When do you require a doctor's note before a child can return to your program? What other adults will be present in your home when you are providing child care? Your policy handbook should offer families information on all of these issues.

- Discuss any applicable regulatory requirements that you need to comply with to maintain your license. Emphasize requirements that relate to infant care. Take this opportunity to explain your experience; any relevant degrees or credentials, such as your training in infant first aid and CPR; and any criminal background checks on you, your adult household members, and any child care staff.

- Prior to enrollment, allow families to spend time in your home while your program is in process. Show parents the infant equipment you will use, and demonstrate how infants are included in your daily schedule of activities.

Discuss goals and future plans. Give parents specific ideas for how they and you can employ the same positive strategies at home and in child care.

- Once a child enters your care, allow a trial period during which you or the family can terminate the arrangement without recrimination. Develop a method of communication with parents so they are consistently aware of their child's day in care. Reinforce the idea that parental involvement is necessary for the social and emotional development of their child. Think about opportunities for parents to participate in field trips, story time, assisting with activities, and sharing information. Give families the opportunity to share in some of the policy making for your program. Parents who feel their feedback is valued are more willing to invest time and energy in establishing collaborative working relationships.

- Take time to think about what would make you comfortable if you were leaving your child with someone outside your family. Employ some of those tactics to make parents feel more comfortable. Always be honest with yourself and your clients. Integrating quality infant care in a family child care environment is often labor intensive. Although many states allow for the care of more than one infant, do not assume that you are automatically equipped to adequately manage the care of multiple infants. You do not want to shortchange an infant or the other children in your program because you are afraid to admit that things are not going as you originally planned. Take time to periodically assess the effectiveness and manageability of your daily schedule. Keep families informed, and do not be afraid to be flexible when necessary.

- Develop a positive relationship and motivate involvement with families by demonstrating your ability to listen, empathize, and provide accurate information and relevant resources. Good communication is built on trust. You are certainly entitled to your opinions, but your opinions are not always as valuable as your ability to steer parents in the right direction. Understanding the resources in your community and sharing information about food programs, immunization requirements, early intervention opportunities, and even the names of good pediatricians are all invaluable.

- Take the time to get to know the families of children in your program. Building trust and rapport is an important component in establishing relationships that work in the best interests of the children. Take the time to understand specific value and belief systems as well as customs that affect the way children in your program think and act.

- Accept that parents are natural advocates for their children. Make them aware of positive ways in which they can exercise their advocacy. Families can be a powerful voice in determining regulations governing child care, increasing the availability of community services and resources, and mobilizing other families. Try to see the families of children in your program as assets.

- Think about the ways in which you currently convey information to parents. The following suggestions demonstrate ways to enhance parent-provider communication:

  - Suggestion Box: Think about introducing a suggestion box in an easily accessible area. Allow parents to provide suggestions anonymously if they choose.

  - Bulletin Board: Place a bulletin board in an area of your home where parents can easily see it during drop-off or pickup. You can post your daily schedule, your menu for the week, any interesting or special activities you have planned, children's artwork, toy and material recalls, and any other information you feel would be helpful to your parents.

  - Newsletters: This can be a fun and creative project. Try to establish continuity in your format and your time frame. If you find that a newsletter becomes more time consuming than you can accommodate, make sure you let parents know that you are planning to stop providing the newsletter and ask for feedback about other options.

  - Questionnaires: Occasionally distribute questionnaires to parents and allow them to submit their preferences and ideas in writing. Remember that when you give a parent a questionnaire, it should be to gather information, not simply to make you feel good. Do not take information you receive personally; rather, use it to enhance your program.

- Phone Calls: If you are having difficulty connecting with parents, ask them if you can talk by phone. Schedule a time that is convenient for both of you.

- Program Visits: Encourage parents to visit your program. Incorporate activities that parents can attend and that children can use to demonstrate their successes. Ask parents to assist when possible. Many family members would enjoy sitting and rocking an infant while you and the children act out a favorite story, for example. Parents may also have specific expertise that can enhance your curriculum. Ask parents about their interests, such as gardening, sewing, nature, cooking, etc.

- Home Visits: It can be very helpful for you to make a home visit if parents are comfortable and you are motivated to do so. Not only does a home visit provide children the opportunity for you to see their home, it also provides families with an important demonstration of your willingness to create lines of communication. This can be a very effective way to establish rapport with the families of children in your program.

- Pictures/Videos: Some providers use pictures and videos to offer opportunities for parents to observe their children in the child care program. This is a great way to keep parents informed about their child's daily activities and accomplishments.

- Assessments/Progress Reports: You can use the developmental milestone information in units 1–4 to assist you in offering important observations to parents about their children during the hours of child care. In providing this information, you are establishing yet another way to keep parents informed and to motivate their involvement.

Partnering with Families of Infants

Those of you who have experienced leaving your infant for an extended period with someone who is not a family member know how difficult this can be. It is important to remember that family involvement is as much a component of quality child care as your curriculum and child care environment. This is especially true when caring for infants. Parents or guardians are and will remain the principal influence on the development of their children. Establishing collaborative relationships with parents right from the beginning helps you create the foundation for positive growth and development for as long as their children are in your program.

In the case of infant care, you are in a position to give wonderful support to child care families. Quality family child care allows parents to go to work or school without unduly worrying or feeling guilty about their children's care. In the case of preverbal infants, this is invaluable. When children cannot speak, parents cannot simply ask them about their day or whether they like their child care setting. Parents of infants are usually in the position of hoping, often with crossed fingers and toes, that their child care choice is an appropriate one. This can be a frightening experience.

Good communication between parents and providers is never more important than when you are caring for infants. Some parents feel that because a family child care provider may be alone, without the benefit of additional staff, accountability can be a concern. Your ability to clearly communicate the daily experiences of the infants in your program can go a long way to alleviate some of this anxiety.

In some cases, especially those of first-time parents, your experience and knowledge about how infants develop are important and beneficial information to share. Your expertise can sometimes be invaluable to parents who do not have the same wealth of experience. Taking the time to inform them about developmental milestones, for example, helps them to become more knowledgeable and prevents them from feeling excluded from many of these wonderful firsts in the life of their child. The ability of infants to form attachments is an important foundation for healthy development. Collaborative working arrangements between parents and providers nurture those healthy attachments. Working collaboratively allows parents and providers to replicate each others' positive behaviors, which should result in positive developmental outcomes for their infants.

Partnering with Families of Toddlers & Twos

In order to forge a successful collaborative relationship, it is necessary to create good communication between yourself and the parents of enrolled toddlers. As toddlers become more verbal, they are communicating how they see their world to you and their parents. Therefore, it is important that you and the parents of toddlers are also communicating.

Consistency at this developmental stage is important. As toddlers become more aware of their world, they become increasingly aware of its inconsistencies. Toilet training, behavior guidance, and social and emotional reinforcement are areas in which parents and providers need to be on the same page. Making the resource materials that you use to develop your curriculum available to parents is an excellent idea. Keeping parents aware of the developmental milestones that have occurred while their toddlers are in your care is a wonderful way to share information and create lines of communication with parents.

How do you as a family child care provider know where to begin in terms of motivating parents to become involved? Often parents who were very involved when their children were infants or when their children initially enrolled do not maintain the same level of involvement as time goes by. Sometimes they may have different life experiences, which affect their available time. On occasion their interest level may change once they become more comfortable with your care. But toddlers usually require more parental involvement, not less. Issues like separation anxiety often occur at this stage of development. You want children to feel comfortable and to develop their confidence and skills. There is no substitute for good communication and active parent involvement at this stage of children's development. Not only does a positive parent-provider connection enhance communication, it also provides for continuity and coordination in children's learning.

Because toddler behavior can occasionally create some challenges in a family child care environment, a provider may find that she is consistently communicating negative feedback to the families of toddlers. If you find yourself constantly complaining rather than collaborating, ask yourself whether you would enjoy establishing regular intervals of communication if you were the parent of a toddler in your program. When establishing lines of communication with parents, it is especially helpful to create balanced communication. Make sure that you are including the funny and enjoyable things that you are watching the toddlers in your program experience. Toddlers are funny to watch and to interact with. Share those moments with the children's parents. Obviously you want to share observations regarding issues that need the shared attention of both you and the toddlers' families, but remember that every parent benefits from hearing some of the wonderful anecdotes that you are able to share with them about their children.

Another of the many attributes of family child care is that some of the children you provide care for are neighborhood children. You are in a position to learn a great deal about services and resources in your area and then share that information with the families who enroll children in your program. This is another way in which you can create collaborative relationships with your toddler parents. Many parents are hard pressed to find appropriate weekend activities for their toddlers, for example. Offer suggestions and share your resources.

Partnering with Families of Preschool Children

Most parents who enroll their children in a preschool program are hopeful that by doing so their child will be better prepared to enter kindergarten or first grade. School readiness is certainly an important component. Keeping parents abreast of their children's progress will reinforce the need for their involvement. Many providers use parent-provider conferences as a means of communicating information about pre-school children in their programs.

As in all forms of communication, it is important not to create a situation in which you are doing all of the talking and very little of the listening. Look at a parent conference as an effective way to receive important information as well as to convey it. To create a curriculum that works well for the preschool children in your program, it is important to get as much information about each child as possible. One of the ways to do this is to distribute a parent questionnaire prior to your meeting. This will give parents an opportunity to think about the information they provide to you about their children. Some suggestions for your questionnaire include:

- Ask parents what they feel is their children's favorite activity while at your program. You may be surprised at the response you receive.
- Ask if there is anything about which their children express concern. Often children will share information at home that they may feel uncomfortable sharing with you. Ask parents to be candid, because this is a good way for you to gain special insight.
- Ask parents what they feel their children's strengths are. Don't discourage parents' willingness to do a little bragging about their children.
- Ask parents what areas they feel their children need to work on. Having their perspective allows you a better understanding of the children as well as

their families. This type of information also allows you to include curriculum activities that are designed to strengthen specific areas of development.

- Ask parents if there is something they are aware of that their children are not currently doing in your program that they would like to be doing. Responses may provide you with constructive suggestions for new activities.

- Is there something that parents would like to see their children doing in child care that is currently not available? This question often initiates important discussion between parents and a provider.

- Is there special information parents want to share that will give you additional knowledge about their children? This type of question not only reinforces your appreciation for parental feedback; it also gives parents the opportunity to become more comfortable talking to you about their children.

Evaluating Your Child Care Program

Because a family child care provider's service can, in large part, be considered the successful growth and development of each child in care, it is important to periodically evaluate your program. The best place to begin is to look at the behavior of the children.

- Have any of the children developed eating or sleeping problems while in your care?

- Are any of the children extremely unhappy when they arrive? Do any of them not show any improvement throughout the day?

- Have any of the children demonstrated withdrawal or accelerated behavior problems?

If you have answered yes to any of these questions, it is important that you talk with the children's families and communicate your concerns. Something may be happening in their children's lives that you are unaware of. In some instances, parents may refer you to their children's physicians. Are there routines or activities that may be overwhelming for some of the children and that may create undue stress?

What about you?

- Are you knowledgeable about and do you understand the developmental stage of each child in your care?

- Do you have proper materials for stimulation and relaxation?
- Do you plan activities that include each child and support each child's continued growth and development?
- Does the arrangement of your child care setting maximize learning opportunities for the children and teaching opportunities for you?
- Do you put thought into your schedule of activities, and is that schedule producing the results you want it to?
- Are you responsive to the needs of all the children in your program?
- Do you periodically evaluate your materials and equipment to check for safety and age-appropriate considerations that correspond with the developmental stages of each child?
- Do the children have sufficient time to explore and experiment in your environment?
- Do the children have sufficient opportunity to play with their peers?
- How is your energy level? Do the children arrive in the morning to find you tired and passive?
- How frequently do you use the television during the child care day?
- How interactive are you with the children? Do you participate in their play? Do you sit at the table during meals and engage them in conversation?
- Does your communication with families allow you to discuss any and all issues, observations, and concerns you may have regarding the healthy growth and development of their children?

By operating your business, you are selling a service. One of the most effective ways of evaluating your service is by observing behaviors as well as the overall well-being of the children. This is particularly important in infant care, because infants are preverbal and generally almost totally reliant on you, their provider, for their well-being. Consistent self-assessment is crucial.

- Do you feel you are sufficiently knowledgeable about the developmental stages of the children in your care?
- Does your daily schedule of activities reflect your knowledge?

- Have you taken the necessary steps to integrate children in a manner that does not exclude or restrict opportunities for healthy growth and development?
- Do you have proper materials for stimulation and relaxation?
- Is your space arranged in a way that allows children appropriate rest and relaxation while permitting you to supervise appropriately?
- How effective are your learning areas?
- Do you have materials designated specifically for each age group?
- As you plan your daily activities, are you including all children in ways that support their continued growth and development?
- How are you incorporating all children in your outdoor playtime?
- Where are the infants during lunchtime, and are there creative ways in which infants can benefit from that learning experience?
- Do you have sturdy and appropriately sized equipment to help infants and toddlers pull themselves up or to assist them in walking?
- Do you have an appropriate collection of books for all children?
- Do you have appropriate toys for each age group? Some toys can be used by all age groups, but many toys designed for older children are not easily grasped or sufficiently secure for infants to explore. Toys that are chosen specifically for infants should be tied to identifiable developmental objectives.

When assessing the successfulness of your curriculum, it is important to look at all the points of contact that occur throughout the day. Are you able to capitalize on all the tasks and activities to make them as meaningful and developmentally appropriate as possible for the children in your care? If not, what do you need to change in your daily schedule or in the organization of your program to create more meaningful and developmentally appropriate experiences?

A good thing to remember is your responsibility to provide quality assurance. Objective and thorough assessment of your child care environment can prevent serious injury or even the death of a child. Periodic review of your curriculum and the environment will also help you make changes to better accommodate the developmental goals for each child in care.

It is important to make sure that your child care environment is safe and hazard free. Mobile children are frequently able to manipulate chairs or stools to climb up to or over barriers. There is simply no effective substitute for your direct supervision.

You cannot assume you can prevent behavior that you cannot see. You must remember that each child is different, and you can never assume that all the children entering your program will respond to your directives about safety concerns in the same manner.

 SAFETY NOTE
A Word about Lead

Lead is dangerous to adults as well as children, but children's developing brains and nervous systems are much more sensitive to the effects of lead. Because infants and young children are more likely to put their hands and other objects in their mouths, child care providers must ensure that there are no sources of lead in the child care environment. Please note that the plumbing in some homes may contain lead pipes or lead solder. If you are unsure about the plumbing in your home, call your local health department or water supplier to find out about testing your water. This is important, because you cannot see, smell, or taste lead, and even boiling your water will not eliminate the risks.

 SAFETY NOTE
Sudden Infant Death Syndrome (SIDS)

SIDS is quite simply a family child care provider's worst nightmare. The thought of having to tell a parent who dropped a seemingly healthy baby off at child care in the morning that their baby has not survived the day is unthinkable. Unfortunately, babies do die of SIDS, and some of those infants die while in child care. It is important for providers to understand as much about this syndrome as possible. The American SIDS Institute (www.sids.org) and the CJ Foundation (www.cjsids.org) are both good sources of updated information regarding SIDS.

In relation to your own policies, it is strongly advised that you discuss your sleeping procedures with all families, especially the families of enrolled infants. Inform families of your napping policy. If you do not have a napping policy, you should create one. Your napping policy should include information on what children will be napping on and where in your home children will be napping. You may want to include your policy regarding quiet options during the nap period for older children, if applicable. If children are using sleeping bags or blankets, you should clearly state who has the responsibility of maintaining and cleaning the bags and at what intervals. You may choose to include information about rules regarding parental visits during naptime.

In the case of infants, your nap policy should be specific and include the following precautionary information:

- Inform families that you position all infants on their backs when putting them down for a nap.
- Inform families that you will reposition sleeping infants onto their back until such time as the infant has demonstrated the ability to roll over independently (approximately four months of age).
- Inform families of your ability to directly supervise napping infants.
- Inform families that you do not allow napping infants to sleep with stuffed animals, pillows, or quilts.
- Inform families that you use only well-maintained napping equipment and that any mattresses used fit appropriately and do not leave gaps between the mattress and the crib frame.

Talk with the families of infants regarding this topic. Stay informed and up to date regarding any information that will allow you to protect the health and safety of the children in your program.

Part 2

The Activities

The activities included in this book have all been used successfully in a wide variety of family child care settings. These home-friendly activities can be implemented regardless of how large or small your child care area. Furthermore, all of the included activities, with only slight alteration or creative additions, can be used to develop additional activities. Remember that while some activities may seem tedious, young children enjoy and need repetition. Newborns and young infants usually will not only enjoy but will gain confidence by repeating simple activities. Doing an activity only once neither produces a mastered skill nor reinforces developmental goals. Repetition is necessary and effective.

Repetition does play an important role in the way toddlers learn. The majority of learning that takes place at this stage is rote learning—that is, repetition through memory, often without understanding the meaning. Reciting the ABCs without understanding what the letters represent is one example of rote learning. These repeated activities help toddlers to become sufficiently competent and achieve success. Every time toddlers succeed and are recognized for that success, their confidence grows. Confidence is a key factor in healthy emotional growth, and these activities are designed to foster that confidence.

Choosing Activities

In choosing curriculum activities, it is important to look at the children who will participate. Understanding developmental domains and applying that knowledge to the individual temperament and preferences of the children helps you create an effective schedule of activities. You are in the best position to understand what the children need from you and your program. A curriculum cannot be produced in a vacuum. Your curriculum needs to reinforce each child's sense of physical and personal identity. For example, the pictures and books you choose should reflect the diversity of your program, including gender, ethnicity, culture, and race. Plan activities to complement the physical and personal characteristics of all the children participating. When developing a curriculum for toddlers, you must understand the developmental needs of each child in your program. It is also helpful to be aware of what realistically can and should be expected of children at different stages. When caregivers do not fully understand children's natural development, they sometimes confuse listless or bored with "good" behavior and exuberant and energetic with "bad" behavior. Understanding child development and having realistic expectations help you support the children with successful activities.

Most child experts agree that each infant is born with a predetermined temperament and a set of talents. No two children are exactly alike, even when they come from the same family. One child may be a whiz with words and the other a whiz with numbers. Every child is special, with talents and strengths as well as weaknesses. Even the most difficult personality has a silver lining. Remember that not all qualities are inherited. There are qualities that you can instill through your caring example and your curriculum, such as responsibility, love of learning, kindness, honesty, and tolerance toward others. Understanding each child's temperament and preferences will allow you to include activities appropriate to the development of each child. Good communication with parents, close observation of the children during a variety of activities, and your experience should help you understand the temperaments and preferences of enrolled children.

You must provide opportunities for all children to learn about themselves and their environment. Successfully teaching children involves capitalizing on all the wonderful curiosity and energy that they possess and creating relevant learning experiences. You should never set out to deliberately intimidate or break the spirits of children in order to produce a result that may meet your needs.

As you become more familiar with the way each child learns and develops, you assess your program for how you can best support the children in their early learning experience. How can you best teach through the type of care you offer? Where and with whom a child spends most of the day can make a big difference. Young children in a group setting may not have their needs met as quickly as a child in a one-to-one ratio. However, there is evidence that demonstrates that children in group settings often learn to speak earlier than children who have not had that group experience. Often children in group child care learn to speak earlier than children who are cared for in their own home by a parent or nanny. You play an important role in this type of early learning. Maximize each interaction with every child by talking about what you are doing and why and by asking open-ended questions that encourage the child to talk—then listen. Each activity and task throughout the day should benefit the children in your program.

For children to fully benefit from each new experience, offer genuine encouragement. You are a cheerleader; every accomplishment should be recognized and applauded. Every child should feel special and successful. When you plan activities and promote play that allows children to be successful and then applaud and acknowledge their success, you enhance your learning environment for all the children enrolled in your program.

In many instances, family child care providers look toward center-based care as a model for their programs. This is not necessary. The family child care programs that are modeled on good parenting practices are usually very successful. In a family, activities occur throughout the day in which all the children partake. In most instances, activities are geared toward the interest of individual children. This model can work quite effectively in a family child care environment, and all the children benefit.

Review the developmental milestones and compare them to the development of each child in your program. These milestones should assist you in introducing activities that will meet the developmental needs of each child. Your most important role is to assist children in their journey forward.

Choosing Activities for Infants

In reviewing the developmental stages of infancy, it is easy to see how important your role is. From the first day of enrollment, you must pay special attention to nurturing and stimulating infants in age-appropriate ways. Seemingly simple tasks, such as responding in a timely and positive fashion when a newborn infant cries, take on additional importance when you understand that crying to gain attention is not arbitrary but rather a significant communication and cognitive milestone. Many behaviors that can be taken for granted are actually developmental milestones that need to be noted and reinforced.

Organize your environment in a way that fosters infants' progress rather than restricts it. Infants who are about to crawl, for example, should not be denied opportunity because it is difficult for you to attend to a crawling infant in addition to the other children present.

Choosing Activities for Toddlers & Twos

The development that occurs between one and three years of age is extensive. Toddlers are normally beginning to walk and talk. As a result, their learning domains include physical and language development. Toddlers are just beginning to form attachments with other adults and children and beginning to experience satisfaction with their accomplishments. Incorporating activities to promote social and emotional development is necessary when developing a curriculum for toddlers. The cognitive development that occurs during this period is amazing. Toddlers are more inquisitive and active than infants because they are more coordinated, confident, and aware of their environment. Sizes, colors, and shapes are meaningful to toddlers, and they delight in using their knowledge to further enrich their experiences. It's easy to include the older children in your program—as they watch you acknowledge the achievements of the toddlers, they will frequently imitate your behavior. Toddlers are learning so many things about their world and how it works that planned activities should offer them opportunities for:

- trial and error manipulation
- exploration of cause and effect
- sorting and classifying
- experiencing all types of sensory materials

Choosing Activities for Preschool Children

An appropriate curriculum for preschoolers fosters social, linguistic, intellectual, and physical development through children's own activity and discovery. It shows them that they are competent to learn, to grow, and to trust themselves as well as others. Your preschool activities should:

- foster social, artistic, and intellectual development in children through their own activity and discovery
- build understanding through repeated exposures and experiences and not through explicit directions
- encourage children to question thoughtfully and think for themselves
- help children enjoy the satisfaction of solving problems and learning skills
- encourage children to begin to symbolize ideas with pictures and signs, as well as spoken words
- promote children to have fun through play, since play is a young child's natural way of working and learning

Unit 6

Physical and Motor Development Activities

Use Senses

✐ Infants Birth–6 months

Developmental Goals: Focus on objects 8 to 12 inches away / React to human voice

Infants love to look at facial expressions. At birth, an infant can see faces and other items best at a distance of 8 to 12 inches. This distance corresponds with the approximate distance from an infant in a feeding position in a caregiver's arms to the caregiver's face. When engaging an infant, try making different facial expressions and sounds to develop the infant's vision and hearing. With your supervision, allow other children to make different faces as well. Some ideas include:

- smiling in different ways
- curling and twisting your tongue
- puckering your lips and making silly expressions with your mouth
- making lip sounds
- yawning
- rolling and blinking your eyes
- moving your head from side to side

✐ Infants Birth–6 months

Developmental Goal: React to sounds / Turn head to both sides while on back

As infants' vision will develop in their early months, so, too, will their hearing. You should note infants responding to sound as well as visual stimuli. Experiment with lots of different sounds.

Always begin by talking with the infants, saying their names and repeatedly identifying yourself. Try to elicit vocal responses from them. If they make sounds, respond with enthusiasm. Let them know that you are pleased, and talk to them about their efforts. "What did you say?" and "Listen to you talk!" are both good responses.

Wait for them to look in one direction. Gently shake a rattle or another safe object from the opposite direction. Note whether they turn toward the sound. Show them the object you are shaking. Tell them what the object is and help them to hold it. Then help them shake the object again. Watch their faces for any change in expression. Try this activity with various objects.

∽ Infants 6–12 months

Developmental Goals: Reach for objects / Transfer object from one hand to another

A great way to reuse plastic bottles and jars is to fill them with different fun objects, such as water, glitter, and food coloring; tricolored pasta; colored water and cut straws; rice dyed with food coloring; beans or other dried food. Make sure the lids are tightly secured. Encourage the children to hold, touch, lift, turn, and shake the containers. Show them how to roll the containers on a flat surface. Watch to see if they transfer the containers from one hand to another. If needed, encourage this by handing a second container to an infant—often an infant will transfer the held object to the empty hand before taking the second object.

∽ Infants 6–12 months

Developmental Goal: Crawl

As infants gain large-motor strength, they will work on using that strength to move about the room. Provide an open area free of small items that could be choking hazards for exploring babies. Support infants in their attempts at crawling by offering words of encouragement: "Pretty soon you'll be crawling. Lift your tummy." Infants may become frustrated when their bodies do not respond as they would like. If this happens, be empathetic: "It's frustrating to move backward instead of forward. You are working hard. A little more practice and you'll be crawling." As infants crawl, talk with them about the textures of the floor, grass, and items they are interested in.

Use Senses

✑ Infants 12–18 months

Developmental Goals: Fine-motor control / Sensory stimulation

This activity can be a controlled activity indoors but can be done more easily outdoors. If this activity is to be done inside, fill a small tub with an inch of soil or sand. Place a small area rug or sheet under the tub to catch spills. If you decide to go outside, use a sandbox or place the tub in a spot where the infants have easy access.

Provide large wooden spoons or shovels and assorted sizes of plastic containers or measuring cups. Let the infants feel the soil or sand. Encourage them to pick some up and let it fall back into the container. Allow them to freely explore the soil or sand with their hands and/or the spoons, containers, and cups, but make certain that the infants do not eat or throw it. Ask them to describe how the material feels. If there is no response, talk to the children about the texture of material.

Alternatively, gather items for water play: small plastic bottles with squirt tops, kitchen basters, and a variety of sponges. Encourage the infants to use these toys with water. They can soak up water with a sponge and then wring out the sponge or suck the water into a baster and listen to the sound when they squeeze the water out into a bowl or cup. Remember that constant supervision is needed during this activity. Never leave children of any age alone with standing water.

✑ Infants 12–18 months

Developmental Goal: Put one block on top of another

Place a variety of differently textured blocks in a cleared area and invite the infants to build towers with you. Model to the infants how to place one block on top of another and describe what you are doing as you do it. If the infants have not already picked up blocks, hand each infant a block and ask him or her to add to your tower. As the infants show interest in the different blocks, talk with them about the textures. "This block is made from cloth. It is soft and squishy." "These blocks are made from wood. They are hard." Continue for as long as the infants are interested.

∽ Toddlers & Twos 18–36 months

Development Goal: Feed self

This is a fun activity you can provide during snacktime or lunchtime. Children at this age are learning to feed themselves, and they are developing taste preferences. Arrange a selection of healthy foods they can eat. Include some finger foods like round cereals, and also some foods they need to eat with a spoon. If needed, help them to grasp the food items or the spoon so they can put the food in their mouths. Talk to the children about what they are eating. Name the foods and talk about them being crunchy, soft, sweet, salty, or sour.

∽ Toddlers & Twos 18–36 months

Developmental Goal: Ride tricycle or other riding toys

If you do not already have a designated space for children to use riding toys, create a driving course in your outside area. Have enough riding toys so that children can engage in this activity simultaneously and not have to wait for extended periods for turns. Typically, toddlers do not yet understand concepts like sharing or taking turns. Younger toddlers will generally ride the toys without pedaling. The great thing about including children of mixed ages is that when toddlers have the opportunity to observe older children pedaling riding toys, they will be motivated to attempt the same. Encourage these attempts while supervising closely. Allow toddlers plenty of opportunities to sit on and move their riding toys along the driving course. Encourage this activity, acknowledging good attempts as well as accomplishments.

Use Senses

∽ Preschool Children 3–5 years

Developmental Goals: Make marks or strokes with drawing tools / Write own name

When preschoolers enroll in your program, have them draw pictures of themselves. Provide a nonbreakable mirror for the children to see themselves. Encourage children to use

as many colors and include as many details as possible. Write the date and each child's name on his or her picture and place them in a safe place where you can retrieve them later. Every four months or so, ask them to draw another picture of themselves. Compare the pictures and see how much development has occurred. As children show interest, invite them to practice writing their own names on their pictures. This is a great project to share with parents.

❧ Preschool Children 3–5 years

Developmental Goals: Use large muscles / Jump over objects

Clear a wide area in spaces with different flooring surfaces. For example, carpet, hardwood, tile, loose gravel, grass, and sand. Place a variety of objects 4 to 10 inches high in each space. Invite the children to jump over the objects. The children should decide on their own which objects they want to jump over. Allow the children time to jump; then ask them to describe how it feels to jump on the different surfaces. Record each child's observations about the floor surfaces. After the activity, compare their observations. Were different words used to describe a surface?

Explore Movement

❧ Infants Birth–6 months

Developmental Goal: Play with hands

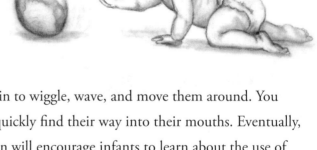

Infants are generally fascinated with their hands. As soon as they realize that they are there, they begin to wiggle, wave, and move them around. You will notice that hands and fingers quickly find their way into their mouths. Eventually, the toes will follow! Your interaction will encourage infants to learn about the use of their hands. Show them your open hand, and wait to make sure they see it. Say, "My hand is open," and wiggle your fingers. Then close your hand in a loose fist. Make sure they are looking at your hand, and say, "My hand is closed." Repeat this several times, waiting each time for the infants to watch the motion.

Now, show them their own hands. If their hands are closed, stroke the backs of them to encourage them to relax. When their hands are open, give positive feedback by smiling and describing the open hands. Then gently mold their fingers and hands into loose fists and say, "Your hands are closed." Repeat this activity until the infants lose interest—often shown by turning away from the activity.

∽ Infants Birth–6 months

Developmental Goal: Move head from side to side while on stomach

One of the first things infants in your program are likely to learn is to recognize your face and your voice. Remember that infants at this age see you best at a distance of about 8 inches. Position yourself so your face is in the infants' field of vision and move your head slowly from side to side. Watch to see if their eyes follow your head as it moves. Next, move your head up and down and watch their reaction. As the infants age, you can move your face farther back.

Gently guide infant hands toward your face. Touch their hands to the different parts of your face. Notice if their eyes follow the motions. Hold their hands to your cheeks and move your head from side to side again. Are they still watching your motion?

∽ Infants 6–12 months

Developmental Goal: Grasp small objects

You cannot have too many blocks in your program. Blocks are a great first toy for children. Choose blocks for infants that are safe and not too heavy. Clear a carpeted area or place a blanket or mat on the floor and set out the blocks. Show the infants the different colors and sizes of blocks. Assist them in grasping blocks. If an infant is reluctant to play, roll or push a block to the infant. Talk about the color and feel of each block as an infant shows interest in it. Build a short block tower. If the infants don't knock down the tower on their own, show them how to tip over the tower gently. Set up the blocks again and encourage the infants to knock over the tower. Repeat this exercise using more blocks. After the infants have mastered knocking down towers, help them build towers on their own.

✑ Infants 6–12 months

Developmental Goal: Crawl

Create an obstacle course for the crawlers in your care. Place baskets or pillows in a triangle or square on the floor. Model how you want the babies to crawl through the course. Get down on the floor and encourage them to crawl to the first basket or pillow. Continue to encourage them throughout the course. Involve the older children by having them crawl through the course too.

✑ Infants 12–18 months

Developmental Goals: Fine-motor control / Stand alone

Make a thick paste by gradually mixing water into two tablespoons of flour. Use a spoon to place a blob of this mixture on a large piece of wax paper that has been taped to the kitchen or project table. Protect infants' clothing with old shirts or large bibs before allowing them to fingerpaint.

Invite the infants to stand at the table. Show them how to move and slide their fingers and hands across the wax paper. Use descriptive words such as *slippery* and *wet* in your conversation with them. Encourage the infants to move their hands up and down, back and forth, and around and around. Use your pointer finger to make some dots across the paper, and allow the children to explore the wet, slippery mixture. Avoid drawing pictures for them, because this activity is meant to promote free movement and exploration. Drawing pictures for the children may inhibit their creativity.

✑ Infants 12–18 months

Developmental Goal: Clap hands

Sit with the infants and encourage them to watch while you slowly clap your hands. Repeat this several times so they become aware of what you are doing. Continue to do this as you recite:

> *Pat-a-cake, pat-a-cake, baker's man.*
> *Bake me a cake as fast as you can.*
> *Roll it and pat it and mark it with a B.*
> *Put it in the oven for baby and me.*

Repeat this several times and watch to see if the infants attempt to imitate your sounds and movement. Focus on the motions and guide the toddlers to clap their hands, pat your hands, pat the invisible dough between their hands, poke with their fingers, draw a B in the air, and put the dough in an imaginary oven. Encourage the infants to clap with you. If you substitute the initial letter of infants' names and use their names in the rhyme, they may listen more attentively.

You may need to gently hold the infants' hands and assist them in clapping. With practice, they will play pat-a-cake spontaneously. Remember: infants enjoy and need much repetition.

Explore Movement

∾ Toddlers & Twos 18–36 months

Developmental Goal: Eye-foot coordination

Establish an area inside that will be safe for toddlers to move a soft ball with their feet. If this is not possible, do this activity outside. Establish perimeter boundaries for them to use when they play with the ball. If the activity is inside, children can push the ball to a specified place. If the activity is outside, they can push the ball to an agreed-upon tree or gate.

Tell the toddlers to use only one foot to push the ball to the designated place. Model how to push the ball with their feet rather than kicking it. When the toddlers have developed the necessary coordination, count how many pushes it takes to get the ball to the designated place. Repeat this activity at various times and change the designated place to add interest to the activity.

∾ Toddlers & Twos 18–36 months

Developmental Goal: Gross motor coordination

Gather several empty plastic dish detergent bottles or soda bottles. Line them up like bowling pins, keeping them close together. Use a ball that toddlers can manage easily, such as a tennis ball. Show the toddlers how to aim and knock down the pins by rolling the ball. Direct the toddlers to use both hands if they appear to have trouble rolling the ball. Have toddlers move closer or further away, depending on their success at knocking the bottles down. Show excitement when they are able to knock the bottles down. Repeat this activity as many times as the children are willing to participate.

Explore Movement

❧ Preschool Children 3–5 years

Developmental Goals: Balance or hop on one foot / Walk heel to toe on a line

Clear a wide area indoors or outdoors. Place a four-foot length of string on the floor, or use chalk to draw a line outside. Invite children to participate in balance-themed challenges. Model how to stand on one foot and exaggerate how you use your arms to help keep your balance. If the children are easily able to stand on one foot, ask them to try to hop on one foot. Provide encouragement if a child becomes frustrated. Next, invite the children to walk heel to toe on the string or chalk line. Ask an older child to show the children how to do this or model it yourself. Allow the children to continue as long as they are interested. If a child loses interest before the group is finished, allow him or her to play nearby doing something else.

❧ Preschool Children 3–5 years

Developmental Goals: Eye-hand coordination / Use small muscles in hands

Spooning small pebbles, Lego blocks, or other small items from one container to another strengthens the muscles used to hold writing tools. Gather two cereal bowls and one spoon for each participating child. It is ideal to place each set of two bowls and a spoon on a small tray to contain any items that spill. Show the children how to hold a spoon by pinching the handle in its middle. Put your right thumb on top and wrap your right index finger under. Wrap your other three right fingers around the handle. Show children how to spoon the items by sliding the bowl of the spoon beneath the items and scooping toward you. As you lift the spoon, hold the spoon horizontally and move the spoon slowly and smoothly toward the other bowl. Pour the items slowly into the second bowl. Encourage children to scoop and pour until all of the items are in the second bowl.

If any items have fallen on the tray, encourage children to pick them up using their pincer grip. This is a great activity to set up so preschoolers can access it without your help. This allows them to feel independent as they practice this exercise as often as they like. Be sure infants and toddlers cannot access the small items.

Interact with People

∽ Infants Birth–6 months

Developmental Goal: Bring feet to mouth easily while lying on back

Prop an infant in your lap in a semi-elevated position so he faces you or lay him on a blanket. Gently lift his feet so he can see them. Softly tickle his toes or rub the sole of his foot. Tell him, "These are your feet." Then guide them back out of his sight and say, "Oh! Where'd they go?" Then show him his feet again and say, "Oh! There they are! There are your feet!" Tickle and rub them again. Repeat this variation of peekaboo several times, making sure you maintain a pleasant and happy expression.

∽ Infants Birth–6 months

Developmental Goal: Roll from stomach

Tummy time is a critical part of all infants' daily schedules. Time on their tummies is helpful in developing the muscle strength they need to roll over. Interact with infants during tummy time. Place infants on a clean blanket and lie next to them or sit in front of them so they can see you. Talk to them and use a rattle or bell to get their attention. Be sure that you vary the side you are on to exercise all of their muscles. Eventually, they will begin to roll over.

∽ Infants 6–12 months

Developmental Goal: Accept being spoon-fed

At this stage of development, some infants in your care may be starting to eat solid foods. An important fine-motor skill involved in eating is opening and closing the mouth. That might seem like a simple task—after all, infants love to put all kinds of things in their mouths! It's not always as easy as it sounds. At snacktimes and meal-times, guide infants to learn the specific steps involved in eating. Show them how you perform each of the following steps, and then help them learn to do the same.

- Look at the spoonful of food and identify what it is.
- Open your mouth to the spoon.
- Put the spoon with the food inside your mouth.
- Close your mouth.
- Pull out the spoon.
- Show the infant the spoon without food.
- Keep your mouth closed until you swallow the food.

Talk to the infants while you guide them through the steps. Describe to them each step you are taking. If an infant keeps the spoon in her mouth, ask her to open her mouth—open your moth to show her what to do. You may have to practice eating many times, but infants will learn more quickly the more you interact with them.

You may also want to position the infants so they can observe the older children while they eat. This not only benefits the infants, but it also gives you the opportunity to remind the older children of how to eat properly. Children love to demonstrate their skills when they know they have an audience. Infants are a great audience.

∽ Infants 6–12 months

Developmental Goal: Follow distant object with eyes

With both hands, toss a small soft ball up in view of the infants. Talk to them as you do this. Encourage them to look up and watch the movement of the ball. Use the word *up* as you talk to them. They should be motivated to look up and watch the ball as it goes up and down. Change your voice's inflection each time the ball goes up and down, using the words *up* and *down*. Give a ball to each of the infants and encourage them to use both hands and toss the balls up. Call the infants by name and recognize the positive attempts they make.

Interact with People

∾ Infants 12–18 months

Developmental Goal: Fine-motor control

Use a small stuffed ball about 6 inches in diameter. (This is a good size so that older infants can easily hold the ball with both hands. Stuffed balls are easier for infants to grab and control, but small rubber balls can be used too.)

Sit with the infants in a small circle on a smooth, uncarpeted area and roll the ball a short distance to one of the infants while talking and encouraging him or her to roll it back to you. At first, encourage the infants to use both hands when they roll. Gradually, they will develop skills and be able to roll the ball successfully with one hand.

For an expansion on this game, a homemade tunnel can be made by using a box with wide openings on each end. Children can also roll the ball under a table, chair, or building block tunnel. Other children in your program will enjoy helping you construct a tunnel and will enthusiastically encourage infants in this activity.

∾ Infants 12–18 months

Developmental Goals: Gross-motor skill development / Eye-hand coordination

Play a game of Simon Says without anyone having to drop out. Invite the infants and older children who are interested to sit or stand in cleared area. Name a body part and ask the children to point to that part. "Miss Sue says point to your nose." Point to your own nose and give the infants time to point to their own noses. Continue naming parts of the body, such as ears, knees, elbows, and ankles. If infants are mobile, invite them to move their bodies, "Miss Sue says turn around." Give older children a turn at being "Simon."

∾ Toddlers & Twos 18–36 months

Developmental Goals: Build tower of three or more blocks / Hand-eye coordination

Blocks are one of the materials that provide many developmental opportunities in early child care. Blocks work well in family child care because they can be moved from room to room and can be stored in a basket at the end of the day. Toddlers love to imitate older children. Encourage older children to build towers with blocks to demonstrate to toddlers how this is done. Make sure that you supervise closely and offer your encouragement when older children build towers. Offer enthusiastic encouragement as the toddlers are able to construct towers of their own. Watch closely so toddlers do not become frustrated or bored. If they are unable to stack the blocks, allow them to find another activity and try again later. While toddlers are building their towers, talk about the concepts of top and bottom. Place a small toy on the top of the block tower and explain how it is on top. Knock the toy off and explain to the toddlers that it is now on the bottom. Repeat the game, allowing the children to move the toy from top to bottom.

∾ Toddlers & Twos 18–36 months

Developmental Goal: Large-muscle control

Toddlers like moving. There is a good reason for this. So much of what they learn at this stage of their development is through activity and play. This is a game that helps toddlers develop coordination and strengthen their large muscles. Invite one or two toddlers to play with you. Take one of each child's hands as you walk and say, "Let's walk. When I say 'stop,' be sure to stop. Ready? Walk, walk, walk, walk — stop." Stop when you say "stop." Change the movement from walking to hopping. "Hop, hop, hop, hop — stop." Keep changing the action, but maintain the same rhythm and always stop on the word *stop*. What you will often observe is that toddlers will soon know the exact time to stop. Other actions you might include are jumping, turning, and marching. Keep in mind when planning activities for toddlers that they need to move!

Interact with People

∽ Preschool Children 3–5 years

Developmental Goal: Use scissors

Small-muscle development takes a great deal of practice and exercise during the preschool years. Invite children to cut tickets from strips of paper or grass from green construction paper. There's no right or wrong way to cut the paper—they just cut. If needed, show the preschoolers how to hold the scissors correctly. Their thumbs should be placed in the top hole and their middle fingers in the lower one. Their pointer (index) fingers should rest just below the rim of the lower hole and provide support to the scissors. As the preschoolers work, talk with them about how they can use the tickets or grass they are making. Then be sure to provide the time for them to carry out their plans. As children master snipping with scissors, invite them to cut on lines, cut curves, and finally to cut out shapes and objects.

∽ Preschool Children 3–5 years

Developmental Goal: Put puzzles together with ease

Puzzles can be made by gluing large, colorful pictures to cardboard or heavy poster board. You can use old magazines, old calendars, coloring books, travel brochures, or you and the children can draw them yourself. Providing one or two puzzles at a time for each child will motivate preschoolers to work with a puzzle. Invite them to trade with each other when they finish their puzzles and have more puzzles ready for them, or invite them to make their own. Use your knowledge of the children to determine how many pieces each puzzle should have. If interlocking puzzles are new to the children, start with a few pieces and gradually work up to more pieces. This activity makes more puzzles available easily and inexpensively, and you can customize your puzzles to the developmental level of each of the preschoolers. When the children develop more skill, smaller puzzles can be made from old greeting cards.

Interact with Toys and Objects

∾ Infants Birth–6 months

Developmental Goals: Follow moving object with eyes / Hold up chest with weight on forearms

After infants can hold up their heads, place them on their stomachs in a safe location, such as on a blanket on the floor. Position them so they are looking out into the room. Place a small, secure, round plastic container, such as an empty spice container, on its side and roll it toward the infants. Observe them. Do they watch the container? Do they reach for it? Guide them to reach for the container, and allow them to touch it. Retrieve the container, and roll it to the infants from a different direction. Help them reach and touch the item again. Be sure to talk to them as you play.

Invite older children to roll the container. Remember to carefully supervise their interaction with the infants.

∾ Infants Birth–6 months

Developmental Goal: Gross-motor coordination

Gently lay the infants on their backs on a clean blanket on the floor or grass. Place a light blanket or cloth napkin over their legs and torsos. Encourage them to kick off the cover. Show great enthusiasm and excitement at their attempts. Repeat this activity as long as they are interested. This activity is good for developing leg muscles and coordination. It also helps infants realize that their legs and feet are still there even though they cannot see them.

∾ Infants 6–12 months

Developmental Goal: Grasp small objects

Reuse an empty plastic coffee canister with a plastic lid. Cut a hole in the plastic lid large enough to accommodate the small items you will use to drop into the container. Gather objects that are brightly colored and are not choking hazards.

Invite the infants to play a game with you. Stand the covered canister on a flat surface and drop an object or two through the hole in the canister. Lift the lid and "find" the object(s). Repeat this activity several times. Then give the infants objects and encourage them to drop the objects through the hole in the lid. They may need a little help at first, but with several attempts they should be successful. Infants will usually enjoy lifting the lid (after you have released it from the canister) and finding the objects. Encouragement and smiles are always good motivators for infants.

✐ Infants 6–12 months

Developmental Goal: Sit unsupported

Infants who are able to sit unsupported are ready to explore the world around them—at least as much of it as they can get to. You need to bring as much of your environment to nonmobile infants as possible. Find safe items that they can practice holding, passing from hand to hand, giving back to you, pushing, rolling, and even kicking at. For example, start with a small, squishy ball. Encourage and guide the infants to try different motions, including:

- reaching for the ball
- picking up and holding the ball
- tossing the ball
- rolling the ball
- passing the ball from one hand to another
- giving the ball to you
- pushing the ball with hands or fingers
- pushing the ball with feet
- following the ball visually when it moves

✐ Infants 12–18 months

Developmental Goal: Fine-motor development

Children love to use their hands, and clay gives them a great way to work with the little muscles in their hands. Find a nontoxic, soft modeling clay or playdough—or make your own with flour, salt, and water. Give the infants small balls of the clay and take an equal-sized ball for yourself. Show them how to pinch, poke, pull, flatten, round, and shape the clay. Guide the infants' hands and fingers to work with the clay. As they gain in skill, work together to make simple clay objects. Allow some of these objects to dry and set them out on display. Show the infants the work that you made. You can also incorporate other items into clay time, such as rolling pins and other safe plastic or wooden tools. Remember: this is also a great time to start teaching the infants not to put everything in their mouths!

Infants 12–18 months

Developmental Goal: Confidence

Sing the song "If You're Happy and You Know It" and invite the infants to move to the music. You can add as many verses to the song as you like. Consider: shake your arms, stomp your feet, shout hooray, honk your nose, knock your knees, and so on. Infants and older children will have great fun moving their bodies to the music, and younger infants will enjoy watching the fun.

Interact with Toys and Objects

Toddlers & Twos 18–36 months

Developmental Goal: Hammer

Show the toddlers how to use a pounding board with pegs and hammers. Name the different parts and show them how to hold a hammer. Allow the toddlers time to work on their own. Be available if they need help setting up the pounding board after hammering the pegs down. Chances are they will repeat this activity multiple times. As each child decides to be finished, congratulate him or her on the effort it took to hammer, and point out to the children how they used their arm muscles in a fun new way.

∽ Toddlers & Twos 18–36 months

Developmental Goal: Throw a ball

Gather a collection of soft balls (rolled up socks work well) and a clean, large basket or tub. Place the basket close to the toddlers. Show them how to toss a ball into the basket. Encourage them to use one hand, but allow them to toss with both hands and either over- or underhanded. Don't create too many rules or the children may become confused or frustrated.

As the toddlers gain confidence, you can move the container farther away. This will offer more of a challenge to the children. Remember to emphasize that the target is the container and not anything else in the room.

Interact with Toys and Objects

∽ Preschool Children 3–5 years

Developmental Goal: Bounce a ball and catch it

For each preschooler, gather a ball that will bounce and mark a place on the floor or outside with tape or chalk. Invite each child to drop a ball on his or her mark, watch the ball, and catch it when it bounces up. Each child should use both hands to grasp the ball and avoid using the body to help in catching the ball. If you count each time the ball is caught, children will find the game even more interesting.

∽ Preschool Children 3–5 years

Developmental Goal: Use small muscles in hands to paste and color

Children of all ages enjoy making collages. The materials you can provide are limitless. As long as a material is plentiful, inexpensive, and not too heavy, give it a try. Allow children to decorate their collages in any way they choose. Link this activity to preliteracy skills by inviting the children to title their collages. With their permission, write their titles on their artwork.

Develop Verbal Skills

∽ Infants Birth–6 months

Developmental Goals: Focus on objects 8 to 12 inches away / Bring hands to midline while on back

Gather simple, colorful objects to show young infants. Gently place the infants on their backs on a blanket. Show the infants the objects and name each item. Talk about how you use them, how big they are, whether they are soft or hard, and so on. Hold an item over an infant's chest and encourage the infant to reach for the object with both hands. Continue with all the infants for as long as they are interested. Repeat this activity often to develop vision focus and support word recognition.

∽ Infants Birth–6 months

Developmental Goal: Hold and observe a book

Read simple board books aloud to the infants. Position the infants so that they can see the pictures as you read. Pause and talk about the pictures on each page before you go on. Hold an infant in your lap and invite her to touch and hold the book as you read. Infants also enjoy looking at photographs of other children. As you look at photographs, talk about what the children in the photographs are doing, what they are wearing, and the expressions on their faces.

∽ Infants 6–12 months

Developmental Goal: Strengthen facial muscles to support speech development

Infants not only enjoy funny faces, they like to imitate what they see. You can encourage this by making funny faces and encouraging movement of the tongue, lips, cheeks, and jaw. Play blowing games using bubbles, cotton balls, whistles, and pieces of paper. As you play the blowing games, encourage the infants to crawl after bubbles, cotton balls, and other items. Supervise closely during this activity and do not allow infants to place any objects in their mouths.

✑ Infants 6–12 months

Developmental Goal: Grasp small objects

There are some toys designed specifically for infants that provide lots of opportunity for developmentally appropriate play. Depending on their developmental needs and skills, you can encourage the infants in your program to try any of the following activities. Using one toy in different ways demonstrates to infants that there are a variety of ways to play with toys.

- Show the infants how to use stacking rings. Stack them large to small and small to large. See if the infants will try to replicate your activity. Talk about the different sizes and how they compare to each other.
- Place the rings on the post. Encourage the infants to do the same.
- Place the rings on your fingers and then place them on the fingers of infants. Discuss how the rings look and feel. Do they fit? Are they too big? Do they look funny?
- Spin the rings. Talk about whether they spin fast or slow and how they look when they spin.

✑ Infants 12–18 months

Developmental Goal: Scribble

As children develop their small-motor skills, scribbling becomes an important activity. Invite the older children to color with the older infants—be cautious about making children feel that it is babyish to scribble. Washable markers, crayons, and large pieces of paper are good materials for all children. As infants gain experience with scribbling, encourage them to use multiple colors. Name the colors in their pictures to help the infants learn words.

✑ Infants 12–18 months

Developmental Goals: Stand alone / Walk alone

Teach infants to recognize and imitate the different sounds that animals make. Use body movements, pictures, stuffed animals, and songs such as "Old MacDonald" as fun ways to reinforce the sounds. Once infants know many of the sounds, invite them to act out a group of farm animals, pets, or wild animals. "Let's all stretch like cats do. What sounds do cats make?" You can also make animal costumes and have them available in your dramatic play area.

Develop Verbal Skills

✑ Toddlers & Twos 18–36 months

Developmental Goals: Small-muscle control / Eye-hand coordination

This is an activity that encourages toddlers to use their pincer grip to pick up small items. Be aware that if there are toddlers in your program who still put things in their mouths, you will need to closely supervise and take precautions to avoid choking. When taking a trip to the park or a walk in your outside play area, invite the toddlers to look for stones with you. They can look for stones that are large, small, bumpy, smooth, or have specific colors. Allow each toddler to pick up and collect a few stones and return with them to your home. Once you return, you can look closely at all the stones, talk about them, and count them. Let the toddlers handle and sort the stones. You will need to decide if you are going to display them, use them for other activities, or put them back outside. If you choose to display the stones, be sure they are in an area where small children do not have access to them without your assistance.

❧ Toddlers & Twos 18–36 months

Developmental Goal: Draw circles

Most toddlers continue to scribble on occasion even after they have begun to draw pictures that are representational. As they develop, toddlers begin to draw specific shapes and pictures. Try to obtain crayons that don't leave waxy deposits that easily rub off paper. Broken crayons offer lots of opportunity for exploration. Encourage children to use the sides as well as the ends of crayons. Doing so enhances small-muscle control and dexterity. As toddlers develop more control and try to imitate older children, encourage them to draw circles. Have them point out and discuss all the things in their child care setting or in their experience that are round in shape. Offer them materials like disks, cups, or stencils to use in drawing circles. As each toddler finishes, ask questions about the drawing and talk about what you see.

Develop Verbal Skills

❧ Preschool Children 3–5 years

Developmental Goal: Use large muscles

Follow the Leader is a wonderful game for preschoolers. Invite the preschoolers to line up behind a chosen leader. Ask the leader to announce changes in activity, and invite all the children to repeat the word as they move. Whatever the leader announces and does, the rest of the children should say and attempt. If the leader calls "Hop," all the players should quietly say, "Hop, hop, hop," as they hop around the space. Before starting the game, remind the children to speak quietly so they can all hear the leader's directions. The leader may hop, march, skip, balance on one foot, crawl under a table, gallop, throw, and pretend to kick a ball. Give all the children an opportunity to be the leader. This is a game that can be played inside as well as outside.

✎ Preschool Children 3–5 years

Developmental Goal: Run with ease and stop quickly

Play a game of Red Light, Green Light with the preschoolers. Invite the children to stand next to each other at one end of a large cleared space. Stand facing them at the other end of the cleared space. Explain the game: When you hold up a green circle of paper, they should run (or walk quickly if the space is not large enough for them to run) toward you. When they see you switch to a red circle of paper, they should stop immediately. Play the game, changing from green to red at various intervals. The first person to reach you can be the new "traffic light."

Unit 7

Cognitive Development Activities

Use Senses

∽ Infants Birth–6 months

Developmental Goal: Explore environment with senses

Gather a soft object for each infant. Show the infants how your hand opens and closes. Show how your fingers bend and how your fingers hold a washcloth or stuffed animal. Talk to them and explain what you are doing while you do it. For example, say, "My hand is closing around the washcloth."

Next, help them open and close their hands and bend their fingers. Gently hold the infants' hands as you work with them. Make sure they are watching, and observe their faces and eyes for reactions. Guide an infant's hands to close on the object you are holding and invite him to hold it. Repeat with each infant, so they each have their own object. Do not expect newborns to hold the object without your help. Remember to talk to the infants while you work with them and to make sure that are watching what you—and they—do.

∽ Infants Birth–6 months

Developmental Goals: Explore environment with senses / React to human voice

Lay infants on your lap or on a blanket on the floor. Talk softly as you touch and name their eyes, ears, cheeks, lips, nose, fingers, toes, knees, and elbows. They should respond to your touch as well as your voice. Gently guide their hands to touch their eyes, ears, cheeks, and so on as you repeat the activity. Infants bond with caregivers in part through touch. Once bonded, infants will find it easier to learn about their environment and develop language skills.

∞ Infants 6–12 months

Developmental Goal: Investigate objects by banging, shaking, and throwing

Gather a variety of objects that the infants can tap on and listen for the different sounds. You can use an overturned pan, a covered shoe box, a wooden box, a piece of wood, a book or magazine, and so on. Place the objects in front of the infants and invite them to explore each object. Then encourage them to tap on each object with their hands. The different sounds should interest and entertain them briefly. Remember that their attention span is very short. As you repeat this activity, find new objects to use, and be patient. Do not force infants to participate if they appear uninterested.

∞ Infants 6–12 months

Developmental Goal: Show interest in playing games

With both hands, toss a soft object, such as a sock ball, up in view of the infants. Talk to them as you do this. Encourage them to look up and watch the movement of the object. Use the word *up* as you talk to them. They should be motivated to look up and watch the object as it goes up and down. Change your voice's inflection each time the ball goes up and down, using both the words *up* and *down*. Give a soft object to each of the infants and encourage them to use both hands and toss the objects up. Call the infants by name and recognize the positive attempts they make.

∞ Infants 12–18 months

Developmental Goal: Practice cause and effect

Lightweight blocks work well for infant activities. You can make blocks out of small milk cartons. Tape the ends together and cover the cartons with sticky-backed paper. Allow the infants to decorate the blocks with stickers. Sit with the infants to play a stacking game. Encourage them to stack as many blocks as possible. Allow the infants to knock over the stack, or if they like, have them build as high as possible and allow gravity to bring down the stack of blocks. Repeat this many times so the infants can practice and discover the reasons the blocks fall over.

∽ Infants 12–18 months

Developmental Goal: Follow simple commands from adults or older children

Play a game of Follow the Leader that includes the older infants. You or the older children in your program should play "follow me" games with the infants as often as they will allow. Make sure your commands include tasks that the older infants can easily accomplish—for example, touching knees and toes, retrieving balls, touching the green blocks. As the infants become more confident, increase the challenges. Observe closely to identify areas where the infants may have difficulty, such as color identification, and incorporate activities that will strengthen this area of development.

Use Senses

∽ Toddlers & Twos 18–36 months

Developmental Goal: Recognize own image in mirror

Have a mirror accessible so that each of the toddlers can look at himself or herself. Encourage this activity and have each toddler name the child he or she sees in the mirror. Take several photographs of each toddler. Hide the photographs in different places throughout your child care area. Have each toddler look in the mirror, then direct him or her to find the hidden photographs.

∽ Toddlers & Twos 18–36 months

Developmental Goal: Do simple sorting

Gather two collections of objects: some that are smooth and others that are textured. You can use fruits, balls, small stuffed animals, as well as pinecones, pieces of textured materials, and clean plastic scouring pads. Ask the toddlers to sit with you to examine the objects. Discuss the difference between smooth and textured. Invite each of the toddlers to sort the objects by touch. Once the toddlers have become confident in sorting the objects, have the toddlers close their eyes. Place one object in each toddler's hands and allow them to examine the items and identify whether they are smooth or textured. Encourage children during this activity and applaud their success.

Use Senses

∽ Preschool Children 3–5 years

Developmental Goal: Sort or describe objects by one or more attributes

Gather enough paper plates for everyone and help them select and cut pictures from magazines of the following food groups: bread and grains; milk and milk products; fruit; vegetables; meat, beans, and nuts. Tell the children to choose something from each category to paste onto their plate.

Place the plates in a row. Encourage children to name the foods on each plate. Tell them that to be healthy, they must eat some of each of these kinds of foods every day. If they are interested, invite them to look for more pictures of foods in magazines and to cut them out. They can then sort the food pictures into food groups and paste each group on a plate.

∽ Preschool Children 3–5 years

Developmental Goal: Put things in order or sequence

Discuss with the children a simple recipe that can be made in the kitchen. It will be more interesting if it's something they like to eat. Some suggestions include:

- make a sandwich
- fix a bowl of cereal with fruit
- make pudding from a mix

Allow the preschoolers to decide what they would like to help you make. Ask the children how to make it and write their ideas on paper. Once the children agree on the steps, follow their directions to make the food. The sequence may not be in order or a step may be left out, but that's okay. They will be watching and helping and may realize their mistakes as you continue with the process. Encourage the activity to be self-correcting by asking questions at each step. Allow the preschoolers to correct and assist one another. Once the task is completed, talk about the result. Go over the correct sequence and talk about other ways to obtain the same result. You can also use this as an opportunity to discuss cause and effect. What changes occur to the cheese and the bread when they are heated to make a grilled cheese sandwich, for example?

Explore Movement

∾ Infants Birth–6 months

Developmental Goal:
Discover hands and feet as extensions of self

Lay the infants on their backs and bring their left legs up so they can grasp their left feet. Place their left legs down and lift their right legs so they can grasp their right feet. This activity will be more interesting if a jingle bell or other noisemaker is attached to each bootie or sock that the infants are wearing. Do this several times and talk to the infants while you move their left and right legs. The sound of the bell should interest them. Allow them to play with their feet and the bells. Then gently lay their legs down. Watch and see if they try to repeat this activity on their own. Be sure to closely supervise and make sure you remove the bells when you are finished, because the bells may be a choking hazard.

∾ Infants Birth–6 months

Developmental Goal: Anticipate events

Gently touch the infants' bare feet. Use a voice inflection that maintains their attention. Begin with the big toe and move to the little toe as you recite the following rhyme:

This little piggy went to market, (touch the big toe)
This little piggy stayed home, (touch the second toe)
This little piggy had roast beef, (touch the third toe)

This little piggy had none, (touch the fourth toe)

And this little piggy cried, "Wee! Wee! Wee!" all the way home. (touch the little toe and gently run fingers up the infants' legs)

Repeat the rhyme several times and many times in the future. Infants will soon begin to prepare for the end of the rhyme when you run your fingers up their legs. If you pause then exaggerate your facial expressions and voice at the ending, they will delight in watching you respond to their anticipation.

∾ Infants 6–12 months

Developmental Goal: Show awareness of object permanence (know objects exist when out of sight)

Place the infants in sitting positions or propped on the floor. Use strips of wide colored yarn or ribbon or narrow strips of cloth approximately 12 inches long. (Remember to always remove these materials at the end of the activity.) Move the strips of material in a wiggly fashion and try to interest the infants in reaching for them. Call them by name and continue to wiggle the strips. Encourage them to reach and attempt to grasp the moving strips. Allow them to touch and hold the strips. Gently withdraw the strips, and while the infants watch, place the strips under a small blanket within the infants' reach. Ask them to find the strips. If they do not respond, bring the ends of the strips out from under the blanket and wiggle them again to encourage the infants to reach for the strips.

∾ Infants 6–12 months

Developmental Goal: Engage in more intentional play

Around nine months, infants are beginning to be more intentional about their play. They may run a train over a track or put things in containers. Use a large container and groups of objects, such as balls, cars, blocks, or stuffed toys, for this activity. Place the objects on the floor near the container. Show the infants that you want them to pick up an object and put it in the container. Encourage them to do this repeatedly. As they begin to crawl, set the objects and the container farther apart to encourage movement between the toys and the container.

∿ Infants 12–18 months

Developmental Goal: Track a moving toy and retrieve it when partially hidden

If you have a small pull toy available with an attached string, you can use it for this activity. If you do not, you can make one by tying a 2-foot length of yarn to a small toy so that it will slide across smooth surfaces. Invite infants to watch as you pull the toy toward a piece of furniture that will obstruct their view of the toy. When the toy is partially behind the furniture, ask the infants to come get the toy. If they can't retrieve the toy from behind the furniture, repeat the activity and watch to see if they are following the toy's movement toward the furniture. If they are not interested, try again later. If they retrieve the toy, congratulate them and repeat the process for as long as they remain interested.

∿ Infants 12–18 months

Developmental Goal: Practice cause and effect

Gather a variety of the infants' favorite toys and at least one small blanket or towel for each infant. When the infants aren't watching, place the toys on the floor and cover them with the blankets. Invite the infants to take the blankets off the toys. Share in their excitement when the toys are revealed. Encourage the infants to cover the toys and invite some of the other children to watch as the infants uncover the toys. The infants will enjoy this activity and want to repeat it many times if you show great enthusiasm each time the toys are uncovered.

Explore Movement

∿ Toddlers & Twos 18–36 months

Developmental Goal: Repeat simple nursery chants and rhymes

Games that include rhymes and movement contribute to healthy development in small children. One of these games is Ring-a-Round-a-Rosie.

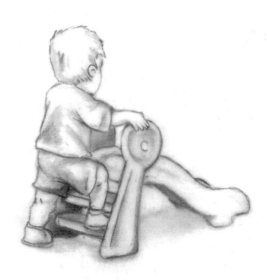

Ring-a-round a rosie, (hold hands and walk in a circle)

A pocket full of posies.

Ashes! Ashes!

We all fall down.

Fall gently to the ground. Children love this rhyme and game. Now play the game again, but instead of saying "all fall down," change the action.

Ring-a-round a rosie, (hold hands and walk in a circle)

A pocket full of posies.

Ashes! Ashes!

Turn around.

You can also clap your hands, hop, or jump up and down.

ᔕ Toddlers & Twos 18–36 months

Developmental Goal: Recognize colors

Invite the toddlers to join you for a game. Ask them to sit on the floor and listen for when a color they are wearing is called. Have colors of paper that match the colors in the children's clothing. Hold up the correct color of paper as you say the rhyme about that color. Younger toddlers may need your help, or ask older children to partner with younger toddlers and play together.

Red, red is the color I see.

If you are wearing red,

Show it to me.

Stand up, turn around,

Show me your red, and then sit down!

Do not wait for all the children to sit, as it may take a long time. Choose a new color and continue with the game for as long as the toddlers are interested.

Explore Movement

∾ **Preschool Children 3–5 years**

Developmental Goal: Show interest in the alphabet

You should be reviewing the letters of the alphabet frequently with the preschool children. This is an activity that helps increase their familiarity with letters. Tell them you have an action or a pretend action for them to do with each letter. Write the letters *Aa* through *Zz* on separate index cards with the corresponding action word written on the back of each card. In preparing for this activity, if you have an action on the back of the card that requires some type of prop, make sure that it's available. Place the cards in a box and mix them up. Invite the preschoolers to take turns drawing a card. Ask each child to read the letter aloud and hand the card to you so you can read the action word. Once you have read the action, all of the participating children can act it out. This is an activity you can do often with preschoolers. The following is a list of suggestions. Incorporate your own actions and change them as the children progress.

Aa Ask a question.	Jj Jump.	Ss Skip.
Bb Bounce a ball.	Kk Kick your foot.	Tt Tap your feet.
Cc Clap your hands.	Ll Look up high.	Uu Get under.
Dd Dance around.	Mm March.	Vv Vacuum.
Ee Empty a box.	Nn Stretch your neck.	Ww Walk.
Ff Fish for a fish.	Oo Open and close the door.	Xx Exercise.
Gg Go around the room.	Pp Push something.	Yy Yell.
Hh Hop on one foot.	Qq Quack.	Zz Zip.
Ii Scratch an itch.	Rr Run in place.	

∾ **Preschool Children 3–5 years**

Developmental Goal: Use positional terms

Create an obstacle course inside or out of doors that allows for different types of activity. For example, you can direct children to go under a table and over an ottoman. Crawling, skipping, and jumping should also be included. Be creative and include positional terms, such as "over and under," "in and out," and "in front of and behind."

Interact with the preschoolers by calling out instructions using the positional terms as they move through the obstacle course. Use furniture, stairs, walkways, boxes, and almost anything else you can think of to create obstacle courses.

Interact with People

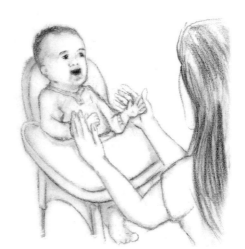

∽ Infants Birth–6 months

Developmental Goal: Respond to own reflection in mirror

Use an unbreakable hand mirror for this activity. Hold the mirror close enough to the infants so they can look at themselves in the mirror. Watch to see whether they smile and coo. If they do, smile or coo with them. Talk to them and call them by name while you look in the mirror. Remember when talking to infants to use an expressive voice. This does not mean that you need to speak loudly; just employ various inflections.

∽ Infants Birth–6 months

Developmental Goal: Discover that hands are extensions of self

Gently lay infants on their backs on a blanket on the floor. Talk to them or make sounds. Watch to see if they lift their heads and try to see you. If they do not, try again. Vary your voice's inflection to stimulate the infants' hearing. Softly press the palms of their hands together. Watch to see if they separate their hands and then bring them back together. As you repeat this activity, you are encouraging infants to be aware of their hands.

∽ Infants 6–12 months

Developmental Goal: Wave bye-bye

Infants often have a hard time making transitions from a family member to a caregiver, and sometimes the same difficulty occurs transitioning from you to a family member. Transitions from one place to another can also be hard. You can support them in their transitions by encouraging them to wave and/or say "bye-bye" to the person, place, or objects they are leaving. For example, when it is time to come inside after a fun time in the play yard, say "bye-bye" to the swing and sand and invite the infant to wave bye-bye. Maintaining this practice helps make transitions easier for the infants.

⚏ Infants 6–12 months

Developmental Goal: Show interest in playing games

Improvise on peekaboo or hide-and-seek. Settle someplace comfortable with the infants, such as on a blanket on the floor. Show the infants a blanket, a pillow, or a large stuffed animal. Then hide behind the item and ask in a pleasant voice, "Where'd [insert name] go?" Wait for a moment, and then look back out and say, "Here I am!" Repeat this activity for as long as the infants are interested. Hide behind different items and move to different spots in the room to show the infant that you will always reappear. Be sure to keep your tone and your inflection light and happy while you play this game.

⚏ Infants 12–18 months

Developmental Goal: Enjoy books, especially turning pages

Provide a book basket or low shelf of books that older infants can easily reach. Select books that are sturdy and are easily handled by little hands and fingers. Encourage the infants to look at the books with you, older children, and independently. Find time each day to sit with them and look at books together. Tell the story or point to and name items in the pictures. Ask the infants to turn the pages. Encourage this activity as frequently as they are willing to participate.

⚏ Infants 12–18 months

Developmental Goal: Engage in intentional play

Find or draw three simple 8½ by 11 inch pictures, such as those of a house, a tree, and a butterfly. This activity will be more successful if the images are large, colorful, and not detailed. A great source for these types of pictures is a coloring book. Invite children to color the pictures with bold colors before you cut them from the book.

Glue each picture onto cardboard (cereal boxes work well). When they are dry, make easy puzzles by cutting each picture in half from top to bottom with only one irregularity in the cut.

Mix the pieces and place them on a flat surface where the infants can play. Encourage them to put the puzzle pieces together. Name the items and the colors.

You can use these puzzles and repeat this activity over and over. The infant will become more confident and perhaps will talk about the pictures by using one word or phrase. Generally it is a good idea to use a maximum of three puzzles at one time. Too many images may confuse infants.

Interact with People

∽ **Toddlers & Twos 18–36 months**

Developmental Goal: Pretend to read

When toddlers hear a poem, book, or song they like, they want to hear it again and again. It is a good idea when reading a story over and over to ask children to tell the story in their own words. Allow each toddler to hold a book and tell the story to you and any interested children. Encourage them to tell their favorite stories, and thank them for their efforts. Another way to support shared reading is to pause while you read a familiar story and let them fill in some of the words. Be sure also to provide time during the day for toddlers to sit and pretend to read on their own.

∽ **Toddlers & Twos 18–36 months**

Developmental Goal: Engage in more pretend play

Dress up is an activity that most toddlers love. Gather together all kinds of clean clothing: hats, scarves, capes, shoes, gloves, or whatever you think toddlers will enjoy. You can engage children in this activity by putting on a hat and pretending you are someone else. As you role-play, you are developing their language skills and contributing to their vocabulary. Encourage toddlers to play dress up by having materials available that they can easily access. When you look for materials for your family child care program, think about different types of dramatic play items. For example, firefighter hats are great props for toddlers. To avoid frustrations, have multiple items available for the participating children.

Interact with People

∞ Preschool Children 3–5 years

Developmental Goal: Match objects with ease

Peg-Boards are a valuable asset for preschoolers. Encourage preschoolers to match pegs to the holes in the Peg-Board. Puzzles are also a good way to allow preschoolers to match up puzzle pieces to their appropriate space. Make your own set of matching cards by cutting 3 by 5 inch cards from construction paper or poster board. Print a letter on each card. Make three or four cards for each letter. Invite the preschoolers to match the letters that are alike. You can also use playing cards and encourage the preschoolers to match numbers and suites.

∞ Preschool Children 3–5 years

Developmental Goal: Engage in more developed play themes

Encourage the preschoolers to engage in dramatic play by supplying props and inviting them to act out different roles. Restaurant play is a great theme to start with, because most children have been to a restaurant. Before the children play in the restaurant space, talk with them about what occurs in a restaurant. Ask them to identify all the people who work in restaurants. Talk about the people they do not generally see, such as the people cooking and washing dishes, for example. Discuss what it means to be a good customer. Allow the children to negotiate as much of the play as they can by themselves. If they are stuck or become frustrated, take on a role yourself to support their play. You might even include this role play during lunch.

Make sure that as you change the focus in the dramatic play area, you have appropriate props to support the activities.

- Restaurant: paper plates, napkins, plastic cups, silverware, tray, notepad, pencils, apron, menus, cash register, play food, food pictures glued to paper plates, telephone, carryout food containers
- Post office: envelopes, paper, pencils, pens, rubber stamps, stamp pad, stickers, cash register, play money, paper and pencils, bag for carrying mail, old hat, wagon for mail truck
- School: desk, bell, calendar, paper, crayons, pencils, envelopes, phone, calendar, and dress-up clothes

Interact with Toys and Objects

∽ Infants Birth–6 months

Developmental Goal: Show preference for black-and-white or high-contrast patterns

Shadows on the wall make interesting shapes and forms for infants to look at. Place a night-light in a position where it will cast shadows from a hanging mobile, for example. You can also experiment with a flashlight. Try making shadow designs with your hands.

∽ Infants Birth–6 months

Developmental Goal: Show interest in manipulating toys and objects

Hold a rattle in front of the infants and shake it gently. As you shake the rattle, sing a song. You can use the tune to "Twinkle, Twinkle Little Star" and make up any words you choose. Engage the infants and make sure they are watching the rattle. Move the rattle to different places, always keeping it in the infants' line of vision. Continue shaking the rattle while you move it and continue to sing. Watch as the infants move their heads in the direction of the rattle. Place a rattle in each infant's hand and sing the song again.

∞ Infants 6–12 months

Developmental Goal: Show interest in objects with moving parts

Hang a mobile or other small lightweight toy from the ceiling above the changing table, close enough for you to touch but out of infants' reach. Make the toy move slowly while you are changing diapers. Afterward, pick up the infants and let them touch the hanging toy. Encourage them to move the hanging toy with their hands. If you can't hang a toy or mobile from the ceiling, hold a lightweight toy in the air while the babies lie underneath. Encourage them to reach for the toy or mobile.

∞ Infants 12–18 months

Developmental Goal: Engage in more intentional play

Gather clean sponges in a variety of sizes and colors. Fill a plastic tub with 1 to 2 inches of water. Invite the infants to hold and feel the dry sponges. Then let them submerge the sponges in the water and watch the sponges absorb the water until they are saturated. Talk with the infants about the change in the feel and weight of the sponges. Wring out the sponges and allow the infants to play with the sponges in the water. Remember: supervise closely during any activities that include water.

∞ Infants 12–18 months

Developmental Goal: Show understanding that objects have purpose

Select several objects, such as hairbrushes, spoons, and cups, that the infants are familiar with and see used on a regular basis. Set the items on the floor. Invite the infants to sit with you near the objects. Pick up one, such as a hairbrush, and pretend to brush your hair. Ask each of the infants to pick up an object and show you how they would use it. Don't get discouraged if they are not interested in your game. Attempt the activity at different times throughout the day. Change objects when children become bored with what you have been presenting to them.

Interact with Toys and Objects

✍ Toddlers & Twos 18–36 months

Developmental Goal: Show an interest in shapes

Present the toddlers with examples of squares, triangles, and circles. Talk about the different shapes that occur in their environment: round dishes, square books, rectangular containers. Repeatedly ask toddlers to identify the shapes around them. When you feel they are ready, choose a specific shape to search for and go on a shape search. Remember to include sufficient materials throughout your child care area so that each toddler has the opportunity to find his or her share of shapes. You can also adapt this activity when you are outside. Ask the toddlers to identify shapes they observe while you are taking a walk. If a child identifies a triangular sign, congratulate him and name the next shape to be on the look out for.

✍ Toddlers & Twos 18–36 months

Developmental Goal: Follow more complex directions from adults

Hide groups of like items throughout the room. Assign each toddler a group of objects (for example, two rattles or three blue blocks) to find. Play this game frequently. Encourage the children to bring the two or three items back to the group at one time rather than one at a time. Applaud them when they successfully retrieve groups of objects.

Interact with Toys and Objects

✍ Preschool Children 3–5 years

Developmental Goal: Develop memory skills

Assemble four small objects and place them in a row—for example, a key, a cup, a toy, and a spoon. Name the objects from left to right, and encourage the children to repeat the objects' names. Ask them to turn their backs to the objects or close their eyes. Remove one of the objects and place it where the children cannot see it. Ask the children to turn back around and tell you which object is missing. If they mistake the object, show them the missing object and repeat the process. As preschoolers become more adept at identifying missing objects, change the positions of the objects for more interest and challenge. You can also add additional items to increase the challenge.

✍ Preschool Children 3–5 years

Developmental Goal: Sort and organize

In family child care, it is always helpful to make practical use of the tasks and the materials you have at hand. One effective way to expose preschoolers to the concept of sorting is to use your laundry basket. Ask children to help you put things into groups. When you do laundry, have the children help separate items of clothing: socks in one pile, shirts in another, and pants in another. If toddlers and two-year-olds are interested, invite them to divide the socks by color. You can also empty a grocery bag onto the kitchen table or counter. Have the children group the fruits and vegetables by type: apples, bananas, potatoes, carrots.

Develop Verbal Skills

∽ Infants Birth–6 months

Developmental Goal: Anticipate events

Hold the infants gently in your arms and rock them back and forth. As you rock, sing a song you know or make up a song. Incorporate the words "I love you." On the word "you," kiss a part of the infants' bodies: head, nose, or toes. Repeat the game often and watch to see the infants' reaction when it is time to kiss them.

∽ Infants Birth–6 months

Developmental Goal: Show preference for black-and-white or high-contrast patterns

High-contrast and simple black-and-white images are the easiest for infants to see. Gather these kinds of images to share with them. Name the object or objects in each picture. Talk about the pictures and tell stories to the infants about what is happening in the pictures.

∽ Infants 6–12 months

Developmental Goal: Intentionally select toys to play with

As you schedule activities for each day, there are often specific toys or materials that correlate with a specific activity. For example, show the infants what instruments are necessary for a musical activity. When the infants appear to understand which toys are used at music time, allow them to gather the instruments on their own. Congratulate them when they are able to collect all the necessary equipment to make music. You can also do this with other types of activities.

∞ Infants 6–12 months

Developmental Goal: Engage in more intentional play

Place an area rug or large towel on the floor and position infants on it, or you can do this outside on the grass. Invite them and the older children to watch as you blow bubbles. As the bubbles fall to the ground, talk with the children about how bubbles move through the air—is there a breeze blowing them, or do they float straight down? If the infants try to reach for the bubbles, blow some close to them so they can touch them. Talk about how the bubbles pop when they are touched. Talk about the colors that result when the light shines on the bubbles. You help infants improve their verbal skills by talking about what is going on around them.

∞ Infants 12–18 months

Developmental Goal: Follow simple commands from adults or older children

Make large circles from red, yellow, and blue poster board. The circles should be approximately 18 inches across. You can also use white poster board and have the older children color them. Discuss colors with the older infants. Hold up each circle and identify the color. Then ask the infants to repeat the name of the color. When you are confident that the older infants can identify the colors, arrange the circles on the floor of your child care area. Call out a color and ask the children to go to it. Praise them when they are able to identify the correct color.

∞ Infants 12–18 months

Developmental Goal: Enjoy books, especially turning pages

Gather a simple book about colors or make one of your own by using poster board or heavy construction paper. Choose simple, bright pictures and glue one to each piece of paper. Coloring books are a great source of pictures that are simply drawn. Attach the pages by using a hole punch to make two holes on the left-hand side of the cover and each page. Secure the pages with a wide strand of yarn. Invite the older infants to sit with you to look at the book. Point to one color in the book and call it by name. Ask the children to look for something else in the book that is the same color. If you cannot find something of the same color, look in a different book or magazine. Continue with other colors or spend longer periods of time with each color.

Develop Verbal Skills

✐ Toddlers & Twos 18–36 months

Developmental Goal: Recall past experiences

Toddlers are generally eager to talk and love it when adults listen to what they have to say. Take advantage of their willingness to talk and learn vocabulary while also supporting their ability to recall experiences. Ask the toddlers to tell you the steps they take to complete a routine task or activity. Have them describe the steps they take to wash their hands or brush their teeth, for example. In the beginning, prompt them when necessary and help them recall each step. Most providers find that toddlers become proficient at this game very quickly. You can use this recall device in many ways.

- "What did we do yesterday?"
- "Tell me what the story was about that we read this morning."
- "Tell me about the favorite game we played outside yesterday afternoon."

✐ Toddlers & Twos 18–36 months

Developmental Goal: Do simple sorting

Understanding opposite concepts is a form of sorting that can be easily introduced in your schedule of daily activities. Toddlers can see that they are little and that adults are big. Point out examples of different-sized objects throughout the day. When outdoors ask children to identify the big and little like objects—big trees and little trees, big rocks and little pebbles. As children become more proficient at this activity, introduce items that are more similar in size, and watch as children attempt to determine which items are bigger and which are littler. Place a group of items in front of toddlers. Ask them to identify the littlest and the biggest items. You can also introduce the concept of size in your art projects. Ask children to draw a small object and then a larger object. Compare the size of block towers and the sizes of fruits and vegetable.

Other opposites such as top and bottom, in and out, over and under, front and back can also be introduced during the course of your day. Take a moment to emphasize the concept of opposites whenever the opportunity presents itself. Recognize the toddlers when they use the words you have been talking about. When they make a mistake, restate their message using the correct terms.

Develop Verbal Skills

∽ Preschool Children 3–5 years

Developmental Goal: Recognize own name in print

Preschool children should have lots of exposure to the letters of the alphabet. Print each child's first name on an index card. Use an uppercase letter for the first letter and lowercase letters for the remainder of the child's name. Guide the children's index fingers over the letters of their first names and name each letter as you do so. Repeat this procedure several times, and then encourage the children to use their index fingers to trace over each letter on their own. Use the name cards as a way that children can take their own attendance. Create an "I'm here" pile or box and an "I'm not here" pile or box. Upon arrival, have the children move their names from the "I'm not here" pile to the "I'm here" pile. When they leave for the day, they should move their name cards back to the "I'm not here" pile.

∽ Preschool Children 3–5 years

Developmental Goal: Count twenty or more objects with accuracy

Involve preschoolers in real-life counting experiences. Ask them to count how many apples you need for snack, how many crayons they use in an art project, how many blocks they can stack in a tower, and how many stairs lead in and out of your home. You can also use counting as a transition technique. Tell preschoolers you want them to sit down for a story by the time you count ten. "Let's count to ten and see if everyone is ready for a story by then."

Unit 8

Communication and Language Development Activities

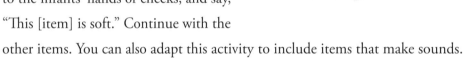

Use Senses

∽ Infants Birth–6 months

Developmental Goal: Make squealing and gurgling sounds

Arrange different types of materials on a flat surface where you will interact with the infants. Gather items that are soft, fuzzy, scratchy, rough, hard, and smooth. Talk to the infants about the items. Ask, "Do you want to feel something soft?" Then touch the soft item to the infants' hands or cheeks, and say, "This [item] is soft." Continue with the other items. You can also adapt this activity to include items that make sounds.

∽ Infants Birth–6 months

Developmental Goal: React to human voice

When your family child care environment provides language stimulation for infants, you establish a foundation for the development of future language skills. In addition to talking with infants during routine care, you can play recorded voices for them. Record the babbling of infants in your program. Play the recording and observe how they respond. Do the sounds excite them? Do they talk back to the recording? Invite the infants' family members to record songs or stories on tape. Play the recordings for the infants. How do they react now?

∽ Infants 6–12 months

Developmental Goal: Develop receptive-language vocabulary

Experiment with infants' sense of hearing. Start by leaning close to them and asking, "Can you hear me?" Watch for a response, and then say, "Here I am! You heard me!" Or, if an infant does not respond, try again. Then move farther away and repeat. Continue to move farther away, and repeat as long as the infants are interested in the activity.

Adapt the activity to their sense of sight. Ask, "Can you see me?" Watch for a response, and then say, "Here I am! You see me!" Move farther away and repeat the activity as above.

∽ Infants 6–12 months

Developmental Goal: Listen to songs, stories, or rhymes with interest

Memory and word recognition develop through exposure and repetition. Obtain a simple book about farm animals. Talk about the names of the animals and the sounds they make. Point out each animal as you name it, and then make the animal's sound. Be animated when you make each sound. Engage the infants in the sounds of each animal. Assist them in recalling and reproducing each animal's name and sound. Repeat this activity often. The animal sounds will interest and amuse the children.

One of the easiest and most fun ways to enhance memory is through song and rhyme. "Old MacDonald" is a time-tested song to enhance memory and cognition in young children. Talk about the various sounds that animals make. When singing the song, invite verbal infants to make the animal sounds.

∽ Infants 12–18 months

Developmental Goal: Grow vocabulary to three to fifty words

Children's worlds are always growing. During the first year, infants are focused on learning about their caregivers, their family, and your child care setting. As they become older, they will explore other places if you give them the opportunity. At this age, infants are learning language skills and forming new connections rapidly. Help them explore each new environment. At the grocery store, take the time to help them pick up, hold, and examine safe items like sealed spice containers, boxes of cereal, and other items. Talk about the items that interest them: Are they big or small? Are they cold? Are they soft or hard? Do they smell? Identify each item that infants reach for. If an item is unsafe, identify the item and say, "Danger, not safe." Then direct their attention to another, safe item, and say, "Here, this [name of item] is safe."

Find ways to engage in this kind of exploration at other locations, such as the park or library. Take walks regularly, and spend time looking at, listening to, picking up, and touching different items. Remember to supervise closely.

Use Senses

∽ **Toddlers & Twos 18–36 months**

Developmental Goal: Show ability to use naming words for objects of interest

One of the benefits of taking toddlers outside each day is the opportunity to talk about what they see. Help them understand how the other senses integrate with what they see by asking questions: What's the biggest thing you see? What do you hear when you close your eyes? What was making those sounds? You will be surprised and delighted by the explanations of toddlers. Let them know that you enjoy these conversations.

∽ **Toddlers & Twos 18–36 months**

Developmental Goal: Increase vocabulary

Help the toddlers understand that there are many different kinds of fruit. Place four or five different types of fruit in a bowl and invite the toddlers to join you. Name and discuss all the fruits in the bowl. Describe the color, texture, and name of each fruit. (This is also a great activity when you take a field trip to the market.) Empty the fruit from the bowl. Ask each toddler to retrieve a fruit, name the fruit, and then describe it. Cut each fruit open and talk about the inside. Does it have seeds, a core, segments? Tell a story about the fruit in your own words. Allow toddlers to tell you what they see and feel.

Use Senses

∽ **Preschool Children 3–5 years**

Developmental Goal: Tell stories

Invite the children to tell a group story with you. You start the story and then each child adds to it as you go around

the group. Some children may find it helpful to pass a prop from one to another as the speaker changes. You could pass a stuffed animal or magic wand. Think about topics that are of interest to the children and be creative. Story starters might include finding a secret fairy who grants wishes, riding a rocket to outer space, taking a pill that makes you shrink, finding a treasure chest, and so on. Keep the story going for as long as possible. If the children do not seem interested in your topic, ask them what they would enjoy telling a story about. Don't get discouraged. Some children who are reluctant to join in this activity at first will generally get involved when a topic sparks their interest.

✑ Preschool Children 3–5 years

Developmental Goal: Pronounce words and sounds correctly

Preschool age children need to learn to distinguish between different sounds. This prepares them for learning letter sounds and blends. Many activities, such as the following ideas, can help children do this:

- Sing songs in which children must reproduce different animal sounds.
- Take turns making animal sounds and guessing which animal the sound belongs to.
- Let individual children recite a rhyme or sentence in a tape recorder. Play the recording and let them try to identify the different voices.
- Say three words, two of which rhyme. Ask children to listen and pick out the rhyming pair—for example, *bell, frog, tell* or *book, take, make.*
- Have all but one child close their eyes. The child with her eyes open makes a sound (with keys, paper, a spoon tapping a glass), and everyone else tries to guess what the sound is. Let each child have the opportunity to create a sound.

Explore Movement

∞ **Infants Birth–6 months**

Developmental Goal: Coo in response to adult speech

Help infants become comfortable with and understand movement. Gently lift them up and down in your arms. Turn around and dance. Carry them from room to room. Walk up and down stairs or around in a circle. As you move with them in your arms, describe what you are doing. If the infants show interest in something you are moving toward or by, stop and talk about what has caught the infants' attention.

∞ **Infants Birth–6 months**

Developmental Goal: Laugh out loud

Hold infants in your lap so that you are able to make eye contact. Change your facial expressions by sticking out your tongue or yawning, for example. Observe closely and repeat when an expression appears to catch the infants' attention. Say a silly rhyme such as "Jack and Jill" and laugh out loud at the end. Encourage the infants to smile and laugh. Remember to try not to startle the infants, but engage, engage, engage.

∞ **Infants 6–12 months**

Developmental Goal: Imitate sounds

Hold a nonmobile infant in your arms as you move around the room or hold hands with mobile infants. Sing the song "Pop Goes the Weasel"

> *All around the mulberry bush*
> *The monkey chased the weasel.*
> *The monkey thought it was all in good fun.*
> *Pop goes the weasel.*

When you come to the word "pop," raise the held infant in the air or have mobile infants lift their hands and arms. Encourage infants to say the word *pop* at the appropriate time.

∾ Infants 6–12 months

Developmental Goal: Gesture or point to communicate

Make up simple songs about simple actions to help infants follow along while you demonstrate motions. For example, show them how to wave their hands and sing, "We wave to say hello. We wave to say good-bye. We wave to arrive. We wave to go. We wave in day and night!" You can make up similar songs: "We walk to go some-where," "We sit to eat our lunch." Be sure to mime or show the action you describe as you sing. Encourage the infants to repeat the actions.

∾ Infants 12–18 months

Developmental Goal: Understand and respond to simple directions

Take walking infants by the hand and walk with them to a room in your house. Tell them what the room is used for. Walk with them to another room and tell them the purpose of that room. Be sure to include the bathroom on your walk (talk enthusiasti-cally about how big kids use the toilet). Make sure they know the names of each room.

After you have returned from the walk, ask the toddlers to show you the first room you visited. Call the room by name. If the toddlers seem confused, take them to the room once again and tell them what the room is. Repeat this process until the toddlers can show you each room, or until they do not want to continue the activity. Repeat this memory game frequently. It may take several days for the children to go to the correct room when requested, but your enthusiasm and encouragement are important motivations for success.

∾ Infants 12–18 months

Developmental Goal: Understand many more words than can be expressed

Cut some pieces of yarn and/or strips of fabric into 3-foot lengths. Ask older infants to help you make a design on the floor using the yarn and fabric. They can line up the pieces end to end or make wavy lines parallel to each other, for example. Show them how to trace the lines with their fingers. Have them follow the leader to walk along the yarn or fabric pieces. Be sure to put away all the yarn and fabric at the end of the activity to avoid the potential of anyone getting hurt.

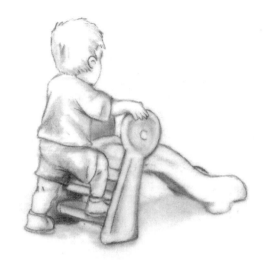

Explore Movement

∾ **Toddlers & Twos 18–36 months**

Developmental Goal: Grow vocabulary to three to fifty words

The primary way young children learn vocabulary is hearing a word repeated over and over in context. When you introduce a new word or talk about something that the toddlers do not yet have the vocabulary for, be sure to repeat the word during the conversation. For example, if the toddlers like to eat apples, you may serve applesauce alongside a sliced apple, while also having a whole apple available as a prop. Talk about the color of the apple and how apples are used to make applesauce and cut apples are yummy to eat. Encourage the toddlers to use the word you are teaching within context. If a toddler points to an apple and says, "eat," say, "Would you like to eat an apple? Can you say 'apple'?" Be sure to acknowledge the child's attempts at saying the new word and never withhold food until a child uses proper vocabulary.

∾ **Toddlers & Twos 18–36 months**

Developmental Goal: Put nouns and verbs together in simple sentences

The ability to sequence is important in communication and language as well as in developing prereading skills. Self-care activities, such as washing hands, getting dressed for outdoors, and brushing teeth, are a good way to introduce simple directions that are in sequence. You can make up chants. For example, chant, "Now it's time to wash our hands, wash our hands, wash our hands. First, we get our hands wet, hands wet, hands wet. Next, we…?" Ask the children what they will do next. If they respond, "Get some soap," then chant that. Add a new part each time.

Explore Movement

✎ Preschool Children 3–5 years

Developmental Goal: Follow three-step directions

Take a piece of poster board and mark it off into nine sections. Write letters or have the preschoolers write a letter in each section. Give one preschooler at a time a beanbag and tell him or her to toss it at a letter. When the beanbag lands on a letter, the preschooler needs to identify the letter and then think of a word that begins with that letter. Explain all three steps to the preschoolers at the beginning of the activity. Encourage them to do this activity independently.

✎ Preschool Children 3–5 years

Developmental Goal: Sing more complicated songs; enjoy fingerplays and rhymes

Try this song with the preschoolers.

> **Swimming** (Tune: "Daisy, Daisy")
> *Swimming, swimming* (move arms as if swimming)
> *In the swimming pool.* (sketch a square with fingers)
> *When days are hot* (fan self as if hot)
> *Or days are cool,* (shiver)
> *In the swimming pool.* (sketch a square with fingers)
> *Back stroke,* (move arms in a backward stroke)
> *Side stroke,* (move arms in a sideward stroke)
> *Fancy diving too.* (pretend to dive)
> *There's no place I would rather be* (shake head no)
> *Than in the swimming pool.* (sketch a square with fingers)

Sing this song with the children and do the motions. Repeat it often so the children learn the words and motions.

Interact with People

✑ Infants Birth–6 months

Developmental Goal: Make squealing and gurgling sounds

When you let infants know you are listening to them and that you enjoy what they say, you help develop language skills and confidence. Begin conversations with them. Say a short sentence, such as, "Look at the children play." When infants respond, mimic the sounds they make. Those simple sounds will later turn into words. As they talk, respond with a nod of your head and a smile. This indicates to the infants that you are listening and enjoying their sounds. Continue with another sentence. Always stop and listen to an infant's response.

✑ Infants Birth–6 months

Developmental Goal: Babble simple consonant sounds, such as "da-da-da"

As you care for infants, engage them in communication as frequently as possible. Introduce simple consonant sounds, then pause and let the infants respond verbally or physically. Sounds include "ma-ma," "ba-ba," "da-da," and "ta-ta." If the infants do not turn away, repeat the sound, pausing again as if having a conversation. Enthusiastically respond to every sound they make.

✑ Infants 6–12 months

Developmental Goal: Respond to own name

Use a piece of 8½ by 11 inch cardboard to draw an outline of a mirror with a handle. Cut a round hole where the mirror would be. Look through the hole and pretend it is a magic mirror. Look at the infants and say, "I see [insert name]." Repeat with each infant. They will delight in seeing your face peeping through the hole of the magic mirror. Allow other children to look through the magic mirror, and call them by name. Continue to do this as long as you have the infants' interest. Lively voice inflection will help retain their interest.

✑ Infants 6–12 months

Developmental Goal: Babble sounds such as "goo" and "gaa"

As infants expand the sounds they make, repeat their sounds and introduce similar sounds. If the infants make the sound "goo," repeat it; then pause and let the infants respond verbally or physically. If the infants do not turn away, repeat the sound and add a similar but different sound, such as "gaa," pausing again as if having a conversation. Enthusiastically respond to every sound they make.

✑ Infants 12–18 months

Developmental Goal: Use gestures and actions intentionally

Sign language is a great way to help infants communicate before they are able to verbalize. Learn a few basic signs and teach them to the infants, always being sure to say the word while using the sign. Once the children are talking, their spoken vocabulary will be greatly enhanced from time spent signing. Here are a few basic signs:

Eat: Form right hand into an O shape. With your palm down, tap your fingers to your lips.

Done: With your palm down, move your right hand back and forth in front of your body, as if wiping a tabletop.

Sleep: Place palm and fingers of right hand along the right side of your face and move your head toward your right shoulder, as if resting your head on your hand.

Interact with People

～ Toddlers & Twos 18–36 months

Developmental Goal: Use a loud and soft voice

Invite the children to play a loud and quiet game with you. Have them join you in whispering a simple rhyme they know. Or just say, "We are whispering with quiet voices." While everyone whispers, you and the toddlers should keep your hands down at the floor. After whispering for a short time, raise your hands and your voice and say, "We are talking loudly with big voices." Repeat whispering and being loud for as long as the toddlers are interested. Make the game more active by raising and lowering your feet.

～ Toddlers & Twos 18–36 months

Developmental Goal: Begin to express feelings with words

Take every opportunity to create activities that encourage children to formulate words and sentences that express what they are feeling. Gather books and/or magazines appropriate for children that have photographs or illustrations of children expressing various emotions with their faces. Ask the toddlers about how different feelings are expressed, such as smiling and laughing when happy, or pouting and crying when sad. Introduce books that represent different emotions, such as fear, anger, surprise, sorrow, and joy. Ask children to describe how the characters in the pictures feel. If children are interested, allow them to share when they have felt the same way as the characters in the books.

Interact with People

∽ **Preschool Children 3–5 years**

Developmental Goal: Answer questions

Preschoolers enjoy riddles, which stimulate their thinking and reasoning. Simple riddles can be developed quickly and are a good game for enhancing language skills:

- Guess what is green and brown and grows very tall. (tree)
- Guess what has four wheels and can take you across town. (car)
- Guess what has a cover and pages. (book)
- Guess what has a head, a foot, and four legs. (bed)
- Guess what has four legs, a back, and you sit on it. (chair)
- Guess what lets you in and out. (door)
- Guess what is round, square, or another shape and holds clothes together. (buttons)
- Guess what is yellow and gives us heat and light. (sun)

As preschoolers get better at answering riddles, you can make them sillier and more difficult, as well as introduce knock-knock jokes.

∽ **Preschool Children 3–5 years**

Developmental Goal: Expand vocabulary

Encourage children in your program to learn about one another, and expose them to stories and pictures about many different people and places. If there are children in your program who are bilingual, encourage them to use their second language in providing new words for objects that the preschoolers can identify. Encourage all of the preschoolers to repeat and use the new words for common objects. Listening to music from around the world is another great way to expose children to other cultures. World music CDs are often available at local libraries.

Interact with Toys and Objects

❧ Infants Birth–6 months

Developmental Goal: Establish the foundation for language development

Listening skills assist with language development. Expose the infants in your program to a variety of sounds. Crunch different kinds of paper in front of the infants. Cellophane and tissue paper make interesting sounds. Make sounds with your mouth and put infants' fingers on your cheek as you make them. Infants find many sounds exciting: for example, buzzing like a bee, humming, popping your cheeks, making a siren sound, and pretending to sneeze.

❧ Infants Birth–6 months

Developmental Goal: Make squealing and gurgling sounds

Young infants are discovering their hands. Take advantage of every opportunity to encourage infants to reach for and grasp brightly colored objects. Talk to them during this activity using their name, your name, and the name of the object. Encourage them to get excited and to make sounds. You can also take an infant's hands and gently clap them in front of the infant's face. As you do this, chant a rhythm, for example:

> *Clap, clap, clap your hands.*
> *Clap your hands together.*
> *Clap your cheeks.* (guide the infant's hands to his cheeks)
> *Clap, clap, clap.*

❧ Infants 6–12 months

Developmental Goal: Gesture or point to communicate

Introduce a collection of stuffed animals or dolls to the infants. Show the infants how to hug a stuffed animal. Then ask the infants to point to which stuffed animal or doll they would each like to hug. Give the infants the objects they point to and encourage them to hug their animals or dolls. Recognize the infants when they respond. If the infants just watch you, hug your stuffed animal again and encourage the infants to do likewise. Continue this activity until the infants respond or lose interest.

✑ Infants 6–12 months

Developmental Goal: Respond to own name

Infants need to learn to respond to their names. You can practice this with infants during your daily activities. Address each child by name as often as possible. Tell the children that it is important for them to listen when they hear their name. As a game, you can start practicing with everyone in the same room. Have the infants sit on the floor while you sit a few feet away. Call out a name and encourage mobile infants to come to you. Recognize each child for listening, and give a hug when mobile infants reach you.

✑ Infants 12–18 months

Developmental Goal: Understand many more words than can be expressed

This is an activity you can do in the kitchen or another room where you may be working. Encourage older infants to work independently in the same room. Assemble and place a variety of items on a low table or the floor. Be sure to have at least one of each type of item for each child. Items such as cups, blocks, rattles, spoons, and small stuffed animals will work well. You will also need a large basket or tub. Name one of the groups of items and encourage each child to place that type of item in the basket. Continue the activity until all the items have been placed in the basket. Have the children empty the basket and repeat the process for as long as they are interested. As the children become familiar with the items, introduce ones that are new to them, such as spatulas and pepper mills.

At another time, place these items in different areas in a room in clear view of the children. Encourage the children to find the items and place them in the basket.

ༀ Infants 12–18 months

Developmental Goal: Grow vocabulary to three to fifty words

Find a box with a lid, such as a shoe box. Make a treasure box by painting your box or gluing colorful pictures on the box's sides and cover. Fill the box with small, safe items from your family child care environment. Sit with the older infants (and other interested children) on the floor. Tell them that you are searching for a treasure. Describe one of the items in the box; then remove the lid and ask the children to tell you which item you were describing. Take the treasure out of the box and repeat the activity.

As the children become more familiar with the game, challenge them to find items by touch alone. Give much encouragement and applause during this activity. If a child retrieves an item that is different than the one you describe, let her try again. Repeat this game whenever the children are interested and willing.

Remember during cleanup to allow older infants to pick up and return the items to the appropriate places. It often takes patience to allow small children to complete a task you could do so much more quickly by yourself. Keep in mind that allowing the opportunity to return items to their appropriate place is also a meaningful learning activity.

Interact with Toys and Objects

ༀ Toddlers & Twos 18–36 months

Developmental Goal: Grow vocabulary to more than 300 words

With the children, decorate a clean box and fill it with interesting props, such as masks, hats, glasses, gloves, small action figures, or dolls. Select something from the box and make up a short story about it. Encourage children to take something from the box and have them tell a story about it. Keep in mind that to a toddler, a story can mean one or three sentences. Applaud them when they identify and talk about their prop. Add words or ideas that will excite their imaginations. As children become more comfortable with this activity, introduce more intriguing props, such as hair curlers, an eggbeater, or a seedpod.

∽ Toddlers & Twos 18–36 months

Developmental Goal: Understand most things said by others

Sit on the floor with the toddlers. Give each child a doll or a stuffed animal. Name simple ways they can interact with the toy. Some examples include

- waving hands/paws
- clapping hands/paws
- clapping feet/paws together
- throwing a kiss

Ask the toddlers for their ideas. Encourage them and applaud their efforts at following the simple directions.

Interact with Toys and Objects

∽ Preschool Children 3–5 years

Developmental Goal: Enjoy learning new words

Like most adults, young children learn best when experiencing something. A good way to help children learn new vocabulary words is to involve them in a new experience. If you like to cook, invite preschoolers to cook with you. While you work, use the words specific to the task. Do not bother correcting the children's mistakes in vocabulary. With exposure, they will learn the correct terminology. If you like to sew, invite the children to sew on burlap with large plastic needles. Here's how to make your own sewing cards:

1. Gather foam trays, paper plates, plastic lids, or sheets of cardboard.
2. Draw an outline of an object to nearly fill the material you are writing on.
3. Hole-punch along the outline you just drew.
4. Cut three-foot lengths of yarn.
5. Dip the ends of each length of yarn in glue and allow them to dry.
6. Double up each length and make a knot in one end large enough that it will not slip through the holes surrounding the pictures.

Show the preschoolers how to move their needles in and out of the holes around the pictures. Talk with them about what you sew and how a sewing machine works.

✴ Preschool Children 3–5 years

Developmental Goal: Retell a simple story in sequence

When the preschoolers have become familiar with a story and feel comfortable retelling the story, make it a little more interesting by creating word puppets. Make puppets from small paper bags or socks. Name each puppet after a word used frequently in the story and write the word on the puppet. You can also use stuffed animals with signs hung around their necks identifying specific words. Have each child hold a puppet or stuffed animal as they retell the story. When the word is used in the story, the preschooler who has that puppet should hold it up. This activity encourages preschoolers to retell the story using familiar words. Encourage children to play this game frequently. As the preschoolers become more familiar with additional stories, change the words on the word puppets.

Develop Verbal Skills

✴ Infants Birth–6 months

Developmental Goal: React to human voice

Choose some of your favorite rhymes and read, recite, or sing these rhymes for infants to hear. Repeat each one several times. The occasional

nonsensical word and the rhythm of the rhymes will engage infants. If you are using a book, show them the pictures that correspond to the rhymes. Their brief glances at the pictures will serve to start associations between books and stories. Recite nursery rhymes whenever possible. Infants will learn to listen. As they begin to talk, they will recite parts of their favorite rhymes spontaneously.

∞ Infants Birth–6 months

Developmental Goal: Coo in response to adult speech

Sit on a blanket with the infants. Call them by name and talk with them about what they are looking at. Pick up items and show them to the infants, allowing them to touch things. You can repeat this activity during daily routines, too. The key is to watch what the infants are interested in then talk about those things.

∞ Infants 6–12 months

Developmental Goal: Say at least one word

Tape a large sheet of paper or old newspaper to your kitchen table or project table. Mix a little food coloring with water and place the colored water in a heavy pan to avoid tipping or spilling. Allow the infants to explore the colored water. As they play, talk about the colorful water, using the word "water" repeatedly. Supervise closely but assist them only when necessary. Encourage older infants to say the word *water,* but never force or punish a child who does not talk.

Alternatively, provide shallow buckets of water and invite the infants to "paint" outside on the sidewalk or fence. There's no need to color the water, as it will change the appearance of the surface, which will delight the infants.

∞ Infants 6–12 months

Developmental Goal: Listen to songs, stories, and rhymes with interest

Infants enjoy touching experiences. Touching usually gets their attention and enhances their interest in an activity. Make up rhymes as you touch an infant's hand. Here's a suggestion:

One, two, touch my shoe. (guide infants' hands to their shoes)

Three, four, touch the floor. (guide hands to the floor)

Five, six, touch my lips. (guide hands to lips)

Seven, eight, you're late! (guide hands to clap)

Repeat this activity for as long as the infants are interested.

✑ Infants 12–18 months

Developmental Goal: Understand and respond to simple directions

Gather specific items or toys and discuss them with the infants. Talk about color, shape, and how each item is used. Distribute the items about the child care area in view of the infants. Sit on the floor with the infants and ask each child by name to crawl or walk to a specific item and bring it back to you. You may have to demonstrate exactly what you want each child to do. Gently guide them until they are ready to follow simple commands on their own. Encourage each infant to find the identified item and bring it to you. Be enthusiastic and acknowledge infants when they are able to follow your directions.

✑ Infants 12–18 months

Developmental Goal: Use gestures and actions intentionally

Singing songs that include fingerplay is a great way to encourage children to perform specific actions intentionally. Songs that work well for this type of activity include:

- "If You're Happy and You Know It"
- "I'm a Little Teapot"
- "Eensy, Weensy, Spider"
- "This Old Man"

Guide infants' hands while encouraging them to sing along. Do each action first so that the infants will understand what to do. You can sing these songs anywhere, and the more frequently you do this, the more quickly infants will become familiar with the words and fingerplay of each song.

Develop Verbal Skills

∾ Toddlers & Twos 18–36 months

Developmental Goals: Understand most things said by others / Use understandable speech

Invite the toddlers to join you in a room that is not too cluttered. Name a small object you think they might recognize. Use the name of the object as many times as you can and give hints, if necessary, to help the toddlers find the object. When they find it, ask them to start a pile of found objects. Continue to name other objects, extending the search to several rooms, if the children are interested. After collecting three or four objects, ask each toddler to choose an object from the found objects pile. Name it again and ask the child to return it to its original location. Talk, talk, talk during this activity. Repeat the words for the objects and their locations.

∾ Toddlers & Twos 18–36 months

Developmental Goal: Put nouns and verbs together in simple sentences

Collect simple books that depict animals or people doing different things. Read a book to the children and talk about the pictures. As you go through the pictures, ask the children what is occurring in each picture. Stress the use of verbs. If a picture has more than one person or animal on a page, ask what each one is doing. Encourage children to use nouns and verbs when they respond.

Develop Verbal Skills

∾ Preschool Children 3–5 years

Developmental Goal: Listen for details

Invite the children to listen carefully as you say two words, repeating one of the words. The children should say the word that you repeat. As

the children gain experience in this activity, increase the challenge by choosing words that sound similar.

- house-lamp-house
- tell-tell-sell
- cook-cook-look
- box-table-box
- three-three-two
- paper-paper-dress
- nine-line-line

- rug-carpet-rug
- child-name-child
- blue-red-red
- fish-green-green
- pot-pan-pan
- boy-boy-girl
- lick-pen-pen

This is a fun activity that you can do inside or outside anytime of the day. Do this activity frequently with the preschoolers. Try to assure that each child has the opportunity to participate.

∾ Preschool Children 3–5 years

Developmental Goal: Enjoy books and get a sense of how books work

It is helpful when you are able to set the stage for a story and capture the preschoolers' attention before you begin to read. Remember to make sure the children are seated comfortably and that they can all see the book. It works well if the children sit with their legs crossed on the floor. Talk to the children about the book before you begin reading it. Name the author and illustrator. Discuss if you have read other books written by the same person. Try wearing an apron with a pocket and hide a small toy or object in the pocket that relates to the book. Slowly pull it out of your pocket to build the children's curiosity about the story. Be creative—use beans to introduce *Jack and the Beanstalk*, for example.

Unit 9

Social and Emotional Development Activities

Use Senses

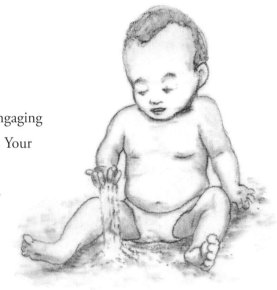

∞ Infants Birth–6 months

Developmental Goal: Track moving person

Throughout this curriculum, the importance of engaging the infants in your program has been emphasized. Your interactions are not only essential for brain development, but also your smiles and positive engagement allow infants to begin both their social and emotional development. If you observe the infants, you will know when they begin tracking the movements of both you and the other children in your program. Encourage this type of tracking activity as frequently as the infant will allow. Be aware when you are in an infant's line of vision. Experiment with different body movements, sounds, and expressions that will sustain their attention. Encourage the children in your program to engage the infants so the infants will track their movements. Try a parade around the crib or infant seat. Watch carefully for the response from the infants—if an infant turns away from the movement, it is a good sign that she does not want to participate.

∞ Infants Birth–6 months

Developmental Goals: Pay close attention to older children and their actions / Respond to smiling with smiling

Sit on the floor in front of a cleared area with an infant securely on your lap. Invite the older infants and toddlers to join you on the floor. Ask the older children in your program to choose a story and act it out. Explain to them that you and the infants and toddlers will be the audience. Gently guide the infant's hands to clap at the appropriate moments. Be enthusiastic. Most children love an audience, and the older children will enjoy engaging infants in their theater. Watch the infants closely. Acknowledge when they laugh or smile, and encourage all the children during this activity.

✎ Infants 6–12 months

Developmental Goal: Play games with adults and older children

Fasten a large rubber band or a piece of elastic to a small safe object, such as a rattle or a small stuffed animal. Tie this securely to a chair, table, playpen rail, or doorknob so the attached object will hang freely.

Show the infants how you can pull the object and let it go. They will see that the object returns to its original position. Pull the attached object several more times while the infants watch you. Encourage the infants to help you pull, or allow the infants to pull the object independently. Continue doing this until the infants lose interest. Be sure to recognize the infants for any positive responses.

✎ Infants 6–12 months

Developmental Goal: Distinguish voices and sounds

Carry a child through different rooms. As you move from room to room, ask questions and provide answers. "What do you see? I see…What do you hear? I hear…" These sensory questions work well in most locations. Be sure that you describe how you feel with each question. "I hear the music. I like music. I see my bed. It makes me want to sleep." Vary your answers to address all the senses.

✎ Infants 12–18 months

Developmental Goal: Wash face and hands

Young children learn from what they see and do. This activity capitalizes on the mixed age groups in family child care. Discuss when it is important to wash hands: before and after eating, after activities, when coming in from outside. Give the older children in your program the opportunity to demonstrate their skills and experience by allowing them to show the infants how to wash their hands. Have sturdy stools available and make sure, if you do not use paper towels, there is a designated hand towel for each child in your program. Sing "Twinkle, Twinkle Little Star" while infants wash their hands. This will encourage them to continue washing for an appropriate duration. When the song is over, the hand washing is done.

✑ Infants 12–18 months

Developmental Goal: Engage in parallel play

For each participating child, gather a large, unbreakable plastic tub. You will also need a collection of small objects that do not pose a choking threat. Encourage the infants to choose objects and toss them into their tubs. Assist them if necessary. Listen for the sound of each object as it is dropped into the tub. Exaggerate the sound when you try to imitate the sound in some manner. Words such as *ping, thud,* or *plop* will help the infants listen more closely when each object is dropped into the bottle.

When all of the objects are inside the tubs, ask the infants to turn their tubs upside down so they can play again. Repeat this activity and encourage them to work independently. Assist them only if they need help.

Use Senses

✑ Toddlers & Twos 18–36 months

Developmental Goal: Show independence in self-help skills

Fill a container with self-help items that are familiar to the toddlers: hairbrushes, combs, rain boots, hats, and so on. Sit with the toddlers to play the game What Am I? When they take an object from the container, ask questions that help them focus on the five senses: What am I? What do I sound like? What do I look like? How do I feel? What do I smell like? Model the activity first, and then have older children take their turns to help toddlers understand what they should do. When toddlers are having difficulty, have older children help if possible.

✑ Toddlers & Twos 18–36 months

Developmental Goal: Show respect for other people and possessions

In family child care, space is not always available for each participating child to have a cubby. It is important, however, that you have a way to identify the areas where children can keep their personal possessions and projects. Labeling can be a fun activity as well as an effective way to identify personal possessions. Have each of the toddlers choose a color. Glue pieces of construction paper in the chosen colors onto same-sized pieces of poster board—make multiple ones in each color. Write the name of the toddlers in large block print on their chosen color. For example, if Kyle chose green, write "Kyle" on each green paper. Encourage the toddlers to decorate their name cards in ways that personalize them. Stickers are great for this.

Place a name label for each child on a container to identify the owner of the contents. While children are learning which container is theirs, have each child wear something (ribbon, button, swatch of material, or a T-shirt) in a corresponding color. Talk to the toddlers about the difference between items that are for everyone's use and possessions that are personal. Label their storage area and their personal belongings. Demonstrate to the toddlers that each child has a color and a name that identifies their personal belongings. You can use your name cards in many ways. Two children playing in the block area can post their name cards to let the other children know they are using the area.

Use Senses

∽ Preschool Children 3–5 years

Developmental Goal: To be silly and make people laugh

Never underestimate the importance of laughter in child care. The children in your program will follow your lead. If you laugh easily and often, and are not above behaving silly on occasion, the children in your program will want to join in the fun. Create activities that preschoolers will enjoy and that will encourage good humor. Try creating a clown school. Supply props such as hats, adult-sized shoes, noses, and anything else you can think of. Give children the opportunity to behave like a clown and make the other children laugh. Guide and encourage the preschoolers by joining in and showing them your best clown routine. Children can also use this opportunity to imitate an animal or tell a funny story or joke. Talk to the preschoolers about the difference between laughing *with* other children and laughing *at* other children. Discuss laughter and how it makes them feel.

‍‍ Preschool Children 3–5 years

Developmental Goal: Enjoy helping with household tasks

Cooking with children can be both educational and enjoyable. When you include preschoolers in a cooking activity, make sure you prepare before the activity begins. A child-sized apron or covering to protect clothing is a good way to start. Reinforce the necessity of washing hands before you begin. Choose simple recipes that will allow the preschoolers to actually participate in the preparation (measuring and mixing, for example). Encourage all the preschoolers to participate. Remember to supervise closely. Give children many opportunities to experience different smells while cooking, including lemon, vanilla, apple, orange, clove, cinnamon, and ginger. They can also smell savory things, such as vinegar, onion, or garlic. Do not allow children to use any kitchen equipment that could be dangerous. You should be the only one to use the stove or oven, and children should understand that the stove is hot and dangerous to touch when in use.

Explore Movement

‍‍ Infants Birth–6 months

Developmental Goal: Show sense of trust

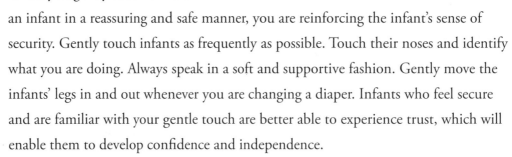

When you gently touch or hold an infant in a reassuring and safe manner, you are reinforcing the infant's sense of security. Gently touch infants as frequently as possible. Touch their noses and identify what you are doing. Always speak in a soft and supportive fashion. Gently move the infants' legs in and out whenever you are changing a diaper. Infants who feel secure and are familiar with your gentle touch are better able to experience trust, which will enable them to develop confidence and independence.

‍‍ Infants Birth–6 months

Developmental Goal: Show attachment (respond positively) to significant adults

Be sure that nothing on the floor could trip or hurt you. Play fun, upbeat music and dance with the infant. Talk to the infant as you dance around. Be sure to support the infant's head and hold him securely. As you dance, use words and phrases, such as *up* and *down*, *back* and *forth*, and *spin around*. Smile and exaggerate your facial expressions as you dance.

∽ Infants 6–12 months

Developmental Goal: Play games with adults and older children

Use a large, round plastic container, a large, flat cake tin, or another open container. Place the ball in the container. Push the ball around the edge with your finger. Allow it to roll freely, but keep it in motion. Encourage the infants to watch while the ball moves around. Stop the ball and place the infant's hand on it. Help the infant put the ball in motion. Talk to the infant while both of you watch the ball move. Continue to keep the ball in motion, and allow the infant to move the ball independently as much as possible with her hand. Encourage the infant to lift the ball and put the ball down.

If this activity is repeated often enough, the infant will become aware of the restricted movement of the ball within a boundary of a circle.

∽ Infants 6–12 months

Developmental Goal: Explore environment (feel safe while exploring)

If you do not have sufficient space to create an infant room, and most family child care settings do not, you should create an infant area. You can establish the boundaries for your infant area by using brightly colored pillows or beanbag chairs. The back of a couch can also be used as a boundary. Make sure there is sufficient space for you to sit on the floor with the infants. There should also be sufficient space for crawling and items that encourage infants to pull themselves up. You need to make sure that your infant area is free of hazards and that the infants feel safe and secure.

Play the Caterpillar game by getting down on your hands and knees and encouraging the infants to do the same and follow you about the infant area. As the infants develop confidence and become more mobile, broaden the boundaries of their play area. Take walking tours around your home and yard. Incorporate treasure hunts and I Spy games as a way for infants to become more familiar with their child care environment.

∽ Infants 12–18 months

Developmental Goal: Begin to imitate older siblings and peers

Older infants love to imitate the older children in your program. Provide lots of opportunity for this type of replication of skills and behaviors. Mealtime provides a wonderful opportunity for older children to demonstrate appropriate behaviors that you would like to see imitated by the young children. Ask children to team up when possible, pairing an older child with an older infant. Give each team an assigned task. Setting the table, placing napkins at each plate, determining the seating plan, and helping to serve the food are all examples of tasks the teams can perform. Designate a "team for the day," and allow that team to choose specific activities. Reinforce cooperative efforts whenever you are able.

∽ Infants 12–18 months

Developmental Goal: To enjoy parallel play

Clap your hands once in front of your waist. Ask the children to clap their hands just as you did. Next, clap your hands over your head once and encourage the infants to do the same. Bend and clap your hands once below your knees, and tell the children to do this too.

Tell them that this time you will clap two times. Count as you clap twice with hands at waist level. Repeat the other steps with two claps.

Tell the children to watch, listen, and clap. Do not speak as you clap once above your head. Did they copy you and clap in the same manner? Assist children when necessary. Go through each position, encouraging the children to copy without verbal prompts from you.

Explore Movement

∽ Toddlers & Twos 18–36 months

Developmental Goal: Show interest in anatomy (name body parts)

Encourage children to move their bodies. Ask them if they are wearing shoes, and ask them to

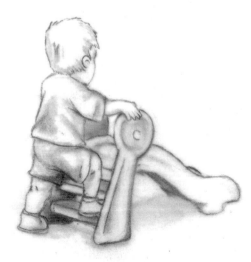

show you where they are. Say, "If you have shoes, jump up and down." Each time you ask toddlers about themselves, point to a different body part. Continue to point out different body parts as long as toddlers are interested.

Other ideas include:

- When you find your elbow, clap your hands.
- Find your knee and turn around.

Once you have played this game a few times, toddlers will perform the actions without your help.

✎ Toddlers & Twos 18–36 months

Developmental Goal: Show strong pride in accomplishments, especially physical

Classical music is a great way to teach toddlers how their bodies move. Select some fast and slow music. Dance to the music and encourage your toddler to join in. "Flight of the Bumble Bee" works well because of its fast rhythm—you and the children can pretend to be bees buzzing around the room. Encourage children to dance in front of the mirror. Allow them to engage in free movement. Play different music during different times of the day. Classical music that is soft and gentle relaxes toddlers and is excellent to play during naptime or free playtime.

Explore Movement

✎ Preschool Children 3–5 years

Developmental Goal: Begin taking turns

Games are fun and a great way to introduce the concept of taking turns. When playing games that include taking turns and waiting for a turn, choose ones that have a quick turn around and do not require preschoolers to wait for long periods of time. The more frequently you play these types of games, the faster preschoolers will develop an understanding of these concepts. This will allow you to progressively introduce games with more rules.

A great beginning game is the Muffin Man. Have the children stand in a circle. Choose one child to stand in the middle of the circle blindfolded or with eyes closed. The other children walk around that child singing, "Do you know the Muffin Man?" Choose one child to approach the child in the center. The blindfolded child must try to identify the approaching child by feeling the child's face. If the blindfolded child does this successfully, the child who was identified goes to the middle of the circle, and the blindfolded child joins the perimeter group of children. Keep the game moving, and assure the children that they will each have a turn in the center if they want one.

∽ Preschool Children 3–5 years

Developmental Goal: Understand limits and rules

Help children to learn how to cross streets safely:

- Cross only at the corner.
- Look left, right, and left again before crossing.
- Listen for approaching cars. Watch particularly for turning cars.
- Cross only in the crosswalk.
- If there is a traffic light, cross only when the facing light is green or when the walk sign is on.
- Always follow the directions of the crossing guard or safety patrol.

You can practice this activity in the safety of your home. When you feel your preschoolers are competent, you can test their skill by taking a walk in your neighborhood.

Interact with People

∽ Infants Birth–6 months

Developmental Goal: Secure attachment

Holding an infant close to you helps them develop trust and secure attachment. Infants need to develop healthy social and

emotional attachments. Infants in your program should be held frequently. Communicate with them by looking into their eyes, holding them close to your body, and responding to their sounds. Hold them close and walk around the room. Stop walking and look into their eyes, smile, and rub noses. Start walking again, and then stop. Repeat these steps several times.

∽ Infants Birth–6 months

Developmental Goal: Establish provider-infant attachment

The opportunity to bond is very important for newborns and young infants. Feeding time offers one of the best opportunities for you to bond with a young infant. Make sure you have sufficient time to sit quietly and feed the infant patiently. This soothing and nurturing routine allows you and the infant to form a lasting attachment.

∽ Infants 6–12 months

Developmental Goal: Play games with older children

One of the many advantages of a family child care setting is the opportunity for all children in the program to interact. For example, infants have many opportunities to practice waving good-bye. Help them wave to the other children in the program. Soon they can do this without your help.

Children love to show younger children how to do things. Model for the older children how to gently play pat-a-cake with infants. Tell them they can be the teachers. Then encourage them to play pat-a-cake with the infants. With your supervision, older children will wave good-bye and play pat-a-cake for extended periods of time.

∽ Infants 6–12 months

Developmental Goal: Distinguish voices of important, familiar people

Sit in a circle with all the children in your program. Place the infant in your lap or next to you. Go around the circle, allowing children to point to themselves and say their names. Allow the infants to attempt this. If they are unable to identify themselves, have the older children point to them and say their names aloud.

∾ Infants 12–18 months

Developmental Goal: Show signs of teasing adults

A full-length mirror is a great addition to your child care setting. Remember that if you use a mirror, it must be secured appropriately. Have the children watch you in the mirror. Describe your movements as you perform them, and encourage the children to imitate you. Help them as needed. Express emotions like "I am smiling" or "I look happy" and movements like "I am bending over" or "I am standing."

Interact with People

∾ Toddlers & Twos 18–36 months

Developmental Goal: Interest in anatomy (name body parts)

Find boxes longer than the children. Cut the sides loose from the box. Ask a child to lie on a piece of cardboard, and then trace the child's outline with a crayon. Remove the child and cut out the outline. Hold the child's hand and use a crayon or felt marker to draw in the eyes, nose, and smiling mouth. Point out the different parts of the body. The child will get the feeling of the movement involved in drawing. Thank the child for helping, and invite the child to name the parts of the face. In turn, children can trace your hand on paper. They can decorate the drawing as well. Allow them to work with the cardboard figure independently. In fact, they may even be interested in giving the figure a name.

∾ Toddlers & Twos 18–36 months

Developmental Goal: Show independence in self-care

Give the toddlers in your program the opportunity to take charge and make decisions.

Model each of these activities many times to help them learn the process involved in each activity.

Encourage toddlers to

- put their coats and shoes in a designated place
- put on their clothing independently
- engage in dramatic play, dressing like adults and playing house, for example
- help set the table
- clean up, placing toys and materials where they belong

Another way to help toddlers develop their independence is by cleaning. Toddlers love to use brooms and mops. Try to find as many child-sized items as possible. Assign cleanup tasks after each activity. Even the youngest toddlers enjoy being included in this activity. Model your expectation and then be patient. Model again when necessary. Allow toddlers the opportunity to feel responsible and independent. Thank them for their efforts and make sure when assigning tasks that you take into account individual competency.

∽ Toddlers & Twos 18–36 months

Developmental Goal: Show interest in outside world

Teaching through the quality of your care includes teaching children about the world they live in. Toddlers are especially curious. Take advantage of that curiosity and supply them with information about their environment. Take walks around the perimeter of your outdoor area. Identify the house and adjacent yards of your neighbors. Identify your neighbors. Talk to the children about the people who may visit your home in the course of the day—the mail carrier, for example. Encourage dramatic play that allows toddlers to dress and act like firefighters and police officers, and discuss what circumstances might bring these adults in contact with children. Take mini field trips throughout your neighborhood and identify the person at the corner store. Allow children to ask questions. If you live in a busy neighborhood, you might sit on the front porch or steps with the children and try to guess where each person who walks by your home is going.

Interact with People

❧ Preschool Children 3–5 years

Developmental Goal: Develop friendships

At the beginning of the year, ask each child to bring in a photograph, or take a picture of each child. Glue each picture to a piece of paper and ask the children to tell you a story about themselves. Put all the pictures together to make a new book, *My New Friends*. Each night a different child can take the book home and introduce his or her family to new school friends.

❧ Preschool Children 3–5 years

Developmental Goal: Role-play

One of the fastest ways to get to know and understand the preschoolers you care for is to observe them while they are playing house. This role-play allows children of all ages to participate, and it gives you an opportunity to observe how the children perceive how a family works. Create an area that replicates a house. You can do this by having the children decorate a large, empty appliance box or a quiet corner of your home. Include as many props as possible (toy kitchen appliances, dishes, small table). When you have completed your area, encourage the preschoolers to play house. Allow the children to create their families without interference. Encourage children to act out their various roles. If they need support, take on a role and ask open-ended questions that prompt the children to think about their roles.

Interact with Toys and Objects

✑ Infants Birth–6 months

Developmental Goal: Look and listen for purpose

Chose simple objects for infants to touch. These can be objects such as smooth ball (chose one that is large enough that babies cannot choke on it), fuzzy stuffed animal, beeswax candle, satin or grosgrain ribbon, piece of wood, playdough, and sandpaper. Help each child touch the objects. Talk about how each of the items feels and how it is used. Note the reaction of the infant to each object.

✑ Infants Birth–6 months

Developmental Goal: Respond to smiling with smiles

Use a large wall mirror or an unbreakable hand mirror and show the infant her face. Call the infant by name and say, "I see [infant's name]." While the infant is still looking in the mirror, use a paper plate to block the infant's view. Gradually slide the plate from left to right so the infant's face gradually comes into view. As you do this, say, "Peekaboo, I see [infant's name]." Repeat this several times.

With the infant watching, try hiding your face with the plate and gradually expose your face by moving the plate. Once again say, "Peekaboo, I see [infant's name]." Be sure to observe the infant's reaction. Repeat this and the other activities at various times. The infant is learning to play a game. She looks. She listens. She responds. At the same time, the infant is becoming more aware of her name.

❧ Infants 6–12 months

Developmental Goal: Explore environment

Place a set of unbreakable mixing bowls and a set of measuring cups. Place the mixing bowls in a row in clear view of the infants. Arrange the bowls with the smallest one on the left. Then move the smallest bowl into the next to the smallest and continue to nest the bowls until all of them are stacked up. Repeat this activity several times and encourage the infants to assist you. Use the words *large* and *small* as you stack and unstack the bowls. Continue doing this until the infant loses interest. Repeat this activity often, and the infant will soon learn to do it independently.

At another time, use a set of unbreakable measuring cups or nesting cups and repeat this activity. In this way the infant will become aware of different sizes and the shape of the objects.

❧ Infants 6–12 months

Developmental Goal: Play games with adults and older children

Practice passing objects back and forth with the infant. Talk about what you're doing during the activity. Use your voice expressively. Use phrases such as "I'm giving you the ball" or "You give me the ball," and hold out your hand. Talk about taking turns, how sharing makes you feel happy, and how you enjoy playing with the infant. Ask the infant questions, such as "Do you like passing the ball?"

❧ Infants 12–18 months

Developmental Goal: Enjoy parallel play

For each participating child, put a lid on an empty oatmeal box or a coffee can to make a toy drum. Give the children wooden spoons or sticks and encourage them to tap on their drums. Allow them to do this until they lose interest.

At another time, sing or chant, "Rum, tum, tum, beats the drum." Repeat the chant until the infants attempt to repeat what you say. This chanting instills the awareness of 1-2-3, 1-2-3, but use the chant instead of numbers for a while with the infants. Then use the pretend drum and tap on it to the rhythm of rum-tum-tum. Invite the infants to tap on the drum while you chant. They may chant with you as they attempt to tap out the rhythm. Allow them to continue as long as they are interested.

✎ Infants 12–18 months

Developmental Goal: Enjoy parallel play

Mix two cups of flour and a half cup of salt. Gradually add one cup of water. Add a little food coloring, and knead this mixture until it is well blended. This mixture will keep for several days in the refrigerator if it is kept in a closed plastic bag.

Tape wax paper to a counter or tabletop. An old plastic placemat can be used instead of the wax paper to protect the work area. Either will make it easier to clean up when the activity is completed. Give the infants pieces of flour clay that can be held comfortably in their hands. Show them how to squeeze, roll, and pat it out. Then allow them to explore with the clay until they lose interest.

If they need more motivation, roll a small piece into a ball and pat it flat. Do the children try to copy you? For further interest and motivation, roll the clay into a long roll and join the two ends together to make a circle or some other shape. Talk to the children about each shape you make. Encourage them to squeeze, roll, and pat the clay while you talk about how it feels.

Interact with Toys and Objects

✎ Toddlers & Twos 18–36 months

Developmental Goal: Show interest in the outside world

Take the toddlers on nature walks throughout the year, not only spring. Walk outside often. Look at flowers, trees, and insects. Stop and talk about dragonflies or butterflies. Observe ants and talk about how they live and work together. Start collections that include pinecones, shells, rocks, and bugs so toddlers can see similarities and patterns. When you are outside, talk to the children about the weather. Discuss the climate. Why does it or doesn't it snow where you live? If you live in an area where the leaves change color in fall, have the children collect a sampling of each type of leaf and compare them. Play a matching game using two leaves from each tree. Go outside after it rains and look at a puddle. If the puddle is on the pavement, draw a line around the puddle with chalk. If it is in a muddy area, draw a line around it with a stick. Watch the puddle throughout the day as it dries. This stimulates wonderful conversations about what has happened to the water.

✑ Toddlers & Twos 18–36 months

Developmental Goal: Show respect for other people and possessions

Keep simple art supplies available, such as scrap paper for drawing, old boxes to cut up for cardboard canvas when using thicker paints or making posters, or pieces of cloth for pasted-up designs or patchwork. Limit pictures to two or three colors to save materials and to teach children about mixing colors and intensities (light and dark). Let children express themselves. A picture does not have to look like something you recognize. Have them practice different techniques, including drawing with lines, shaping figures, and designing with blocks of color. They can also experiment by using contrasting colors and shades.

Display the children's art in your home. Some providers decorate the foyers of their homes with the art created by the children in their programs. You can periodically mount pictures, place them in glass-covered frames, and hang them in your entryway. The result can be truly amazing. Not only are the pictures colorful and actually quite lovely in their frames, but the children will be proud of their artwork and how it is presented. You can change the artwork every month. The children will come to anticipate each new art show.

Interact with Toys and Objects

∽ Preschool Children 3–5 years

Developmental Goal: Play with peers

One of the ways preschoolers develop social and emotional confidence is to work cooperatively and successfully with one another, as well as with the materials and equipment you include in your family child care environment. Give each preschooler three small balls of playdough: one red, one blue, and one yellow. Encourage them to pinch off small pieces and squeeze them together to make new colors. Always encourage collaboration. Guide children to share ideas and assist one another. You can also fill clear plastic cups with water and encourage the children to experiment and make different colors with food coloring. Applaud their success and talk to them about the benefits of working together in a group.

∽ Preschool Children 3–5 years

Developmental Goals: Show pride in work / Increase attention span

Some artists create art from all kinds of unused items, including things they have found on the beach or even in the backyard. In family child care, it is possible to collect all types of materials and involve all of the children in the process. Toddlers will love going on an adventure, and infants will benefit from observing all the action. It is important to remember that with multiage groups, a provider always needs to be aware of hazardous objects. Check all outdoor space used by the children in your program for possible hazards prior to beginning your search.

Go on a treasure hunt outside to find things that can be used in a collage, such as sticks and leaves, flowers to be pressed, feathers, pebbles, and shells. You can also hunt inside for other things, such as scraps of paper, buttons, pieces of cloth, and ribbons. Look for some heavy cardboard or wood to use as backing. Have the children lay out the materials in a design on the backing. Let them move things around until they like their design. Use heavy-duty glue, and supervise the children while they glue the items on the backing.

Develop Verbal Skills

∽ Infants Birth–6 months

Developmental Goal: Smile at the sound of familiar voices

Allow the older children to approach infants when they are awake and lying in their cribs or infant seats. With your guidance, encourage the children to smile and introduce themselves. Infants often respond to other children enthusiastically. Repeat these introductions often and encourage the older children to talk to the infants at other times as well.

∽ Infants Birth–6 months

Developmental Goal: Babble and laugh to get adult attention

Because young infants are nonverbal, it is important for you to take advantage of those moments when an infant is attempting to get your attention. You need to be watching so that you become familiar with each infant's cues. Remember that no two infants are exactly alike. When infants become excited and kick their feet and move their arms, they are usually letting you know that they are ready to play. Whenever possible, respond to those cues with enthusiasm and positive energy. Try the finger game. Hold the infant in your lap or lay him on his back. Put your index finger in the infant's hand. The infant will probably grasp your finger, as this is a natural reflex. While the infant is grasping your finger, make eye contact. Smile and talk with an inflected voice. As infants become more excited with the game, match their enthusiasm with your own. Stay connected for as long as the infant will allow.

∽ Infants 6–12 months

Developmental Goal: Distinguish voice tones and emotions

Review your day in song. Make up a tune and sing about what occurred during the day. Sing about things like waking up, getting dressed, eating breakfast, coming to child care, etc. You can also sing about the people in the infants' life during the day. You can sing about the other children in the program, a participating household member or assistant, or the pets. Sing your songs and engage each infant while you sing. It's fun to personalize what you sing about so that each infant knows you are singing about him.

∽ Infants 6–12 months

Developmental Goal: Play game with adults and older children

Infants are beginning to connect simple words with actions. Use words to name concepts and feelings whenever possible. Write concept words on 3 by 5 inch cards: words such as *sad, happy, share,* and *kindness.* Ask the older children to choose a card and act out the word on the card. Involve the infants by guiding them to watch what the older children are doing. Frequently say each word and connect it to the action.

∽ Infants 12–18 months

Developmental Goal: Enjoy parallel play

Obtain a large box. Draw and cut a door large enough for children to go in and out of easily. If you want the door to open and close, leave the left side of the drawn door intact. A doorknob can be made from a spool fastened with a long bolt that fits through the spool and the cardboard and is secured by a nut. Use masking tape over any rough edges. Draw and cut out two or more windows, and encourage children to help decorate the outside of the house with felt markers.

Invite them to move into the new house. Teach them the names of the different parts of the house: *door, window, roof, wall, doorknob,* and so on. Once they become familiar with the house, they will enjoy going in and out. Use the words *in, out, open,* and *close.* Infants may begin to carry objects back and forth to their new house, as children of this age enjoy carrying objects around.

∽ Infants 12–18 months

Developmental Goal: Begin to imitate

Books are an important part of social and emotional development. Choose books that have simple stories and pictures of familiar objects and places. Have children look at books in pairs. Pairing older children with toddlers can be a great asset in this activity. Encourage them to take turns talking about the pictures or making up stories. Initially, you may find that the older child does most of the talking, but over time, toddlers are usually eager to demonstrate their verbal skills.

Develop Verbal Skills

∽ Toddlers & Twos 18–36 months

Developmental Goal: Identify and talk about others' feelings

Show the toddlers photographs of faces. Include a picture of each child. Spread out the pictures and have the toddlers find photographs of themselves. Find a picture of a child's face that looks happy. Ask all the children to make a happy face. Keep looking for happy face photographs. On another day, look for different kinds of expressions, such as excited, sad, and silly. Ask the children to describe the expressions on the faces in the photographs.

∞ Toddlers & Twos 18–36 months

Developmental Goal: Identify and talk about personal feelings

Can You Do It Too? is a game that allows toddlers to identify their feelings. Make a happy or sad face. Ask the toddlers what they think your facial expression means. Talk to them about why they think your expression is happy or sad. Ask them about what makes them happy or sad. Invite them to pretend to be happy or sad. Use this as an opportunity to discuss feelings. As the toddlers become more confident with this game, you may include feelings such as anger, drowsiness, and surprise. Encourage the toddlers to role-play. Sing a song about feelings to the tune of "Old MacDonald." For example

> *Sarah is sometimes sad*
> *and when she's sad, she says* _____

Add sounds as directed by the toddlers. Continue with other feelings.

Develop Verbal Skills

∞ Preschool Children 3–5 years

Developmental Goal: Play with peers

Through dramatic play, children learn cooperative play, improve social skills, and develop impulse control while they release emotions, practice language skills, and express themselves creatively. Here are some suggestions for dramatic play areas that will delight children:

- grocery store
- hospital
- shoe store
- travel agency

- beauty parlor
- post office
- theater
- airport
- fire or police station
- school
- pet shop
- restaurant
- office

∽ Preschool Children 3–5 years

Developmental Goal: Increase attention span

Recite a rhyme or fingerplay and leave out a word. Ask children to identify the missing word. Have them close their eyes. Tell them to raise their hand when they hear a sound and to lower their hand when it stops. Use a xylophone or other musical instrument to make the sound. Take children on a listening walk in the building or outside. When you return, ask them to identify all the different sounds they heard.

Part

3

Your Program and Practices

The first part of this curriculum covers child development and quality care for children. The second part provides activities. This third part completes the curriculum by giving an overview of a variety of topics that are central to quality care. The day-to-day operations and choices you make impact your quality of care. You may find information in the following pages of which you have not been aware, or the answer to a question you might have.

Sample Daily Schedules

Infants

Arrival time: Provider should be prepared to hold infant at time of arrival.

Tummy time: Allow infant to lie on blanket with a few soft toys during circle or group time.

Feeding: Provider should always hold infants during feeding.

Diapering: Use this time for conversation, games likes peekaboo, and eye contact.

Naptime: Follow the infants' cues to know when they are tired.

Sit up time: Use infant seats or high chairs and allow infants to grasp and handle toys on the tray.

Outside time: Provider should include infants in outdoor activity.

Diapering

Feeding

Opportunity for play: Choose an activity from the curriculum to guide the infants' playtime.

Diapering

Feeding

Naptime, if neeeded

Opportunity for play

Departure: Provider should always greet family members, report on the infants' day, and say good-bye to the infants.

Toddlers and Twos

Arrival time: Provider should always greet the family and the child.

Free play: Set up blocks, dramatic play, and manipulatives for children to choose from.

Hand washing: Talk about how and why everyone should wash their hands.

Breakfast: Sit and talk with the children while eating.

Bathroom: Include brushing teeth.

Opportunity for play: Choose an activity from the curriculum to guide the toddlers' playtime. Also, supply playdough, paper and crayons, puzzles, etc., for exploration and creativity.

Story time: Read favorite books and introduce new stories.

Bathroom: Allow the children as much independence as they are ready for.

Outside time: Discuss science in nature and math during your outside play: gathering leaves, observing cloud formations, counting while the ball bounces, etc.

Hand washing

Lunch

Bathroom: Include brushing teeth.

Naptime

Activity: After nap is a great time to choose a physical activity from the curriculum.

Free play: Make sure sufficient materials are available so toddlers do not have to wait for extended periods.

Outside time

Bathroom

Story time: Choose a story that allows children to act out roles.

Departure: Provider should always greet family members, report on the toddler's day, and say good-bye to the toddlers.

Preschool Children

Arrival time: Provider should always greet the family and the child.

Free play: Set up blocks, dramatic play, and manipulatives for children to choose from.

Hand washing: Talk about how and why everyone should wash their hands.

Breakfast: Include both conversation and assigned tasks: setting table, cleanup, etc.

Group time: This time can be used to introduce your daily schedule and any other activities that are sufficiently inclusive for all the children in your group.

Activity time: Choose activities from the curriculum. This period can include art, blocks, dramatic play, fine-motor, story time, music, sand/water, science/discovery, and other activities, such as cooking.

Cleanup: Make this time fun by singing and playing word games during cleanup.

Outdoor activity: Your time outside can include free play as well as planned activities, such as games that develop gross-motor skills.

Bathroom

Lunch

Cleanup

Bathroom

Nap or quiet time

Snacks

Group time: Include stories, dramatic play, music, and conversation about the day.

Departure: Provider should always greet family members, report on news of the day, and say good-bye to the child.

Guiding Children's Behavior

Communicating with families is essential when you are creating strategies for guiding behavior. You should know which type of behavior guidance each family uses at home. When misbehavior, such as biting, becomes chronic, you and the child's family must respond in a consistent manner.

Discussing misbehavior with a child's family can be challenging. Here are some tips to support you as you prepare to discuss challenging topics with families.

- Practice. Think about what you intend to say before you say it.
- Document events that have caused concern. This helps you present an organized chronology of events.
- During your pre-enrollment interview with families, discuss methods of dealing with specific behaviors. Ask how they deal with behavioral issues at home.
- Remember that the two most common responses from families when confronted with their children's misbehavior are "He never does that at home" and "Where were you when she did that?" It's important to be prepared to respond professionally. If it is true a child is presenting behaviors in family child care that are not presented at home, why? "Where were you?" is a valid question. If a child is consistently injuring himself or other children or disrupting the activities while in your care, you need to examine your role and think about how you can better support this child.

Below are common discipline strategies with suggestions on how to guide children's behavior without using punitive measures.

Natural Consequences

Understanding natural consequences helps young children make the connection between their behavior and how it affects them and the people around them. A natural consequence of a child refusing to eat snack is that the child will be hungry at dinner. Thus, not all natural consequences are negative. Many, such as this example, help children understand how their choices affect them. Other times, natural consequences involve other people. Then children learn that how people respond to them is often directly related to their own behavior. When you respond to a child's behavior, it is important to stay calm and maintain a moderate tone of voice while letting a child know that you are displeased with the behavior. Focus your comments on the behavior—not the child.

Distraction

For children under the age of three, distraction is the most frequently used technique for redirecting behavior. In a group of multiage children, younger ones often seek attention and want to participate but do not know how. Their behavior can disrupt the older children's activities. When planning activities for older children, make sure younger children are involved in an age-appropriate activity. Remember your obligation to provide curriculum for all the ages and abilities of children in your program. Distracting young children with positive redirection, including a variety of alternate activities or toys, can be an effective way of dealing with disruptive behavior.

Eye Contact, also Known as "The Look"

Many providers find that when they look directly at misbehaving children, the children cease the negative behavior. The goal, however, is not to make them fearful of you. On the contrary, if you are using eye contact appropriately, children in your program will respond positively. Children do not want to be noticed when they know they are doing something they shouldn't by the person they most want to please.

Time-Outs

Time-outs should be used sparingly and never with children under three. The amount of time children sit in time-outs should not be more than their age in minutes. You should always be able to see children during their time-outs. They should never be humiliated or scorned—for example, placed in a corner facing the wall. If time-outs are used too frequently, they quickly lose their effectiveness. They have become ineffective if, for example, a child begins to act disruptively and before the provider says a word, he smiles and walks over to the time-out chair to sit down.

"Say It"

Verbalizing feelings is a valuable skill for young children to develop. They need repeated coaching to develop this skill. You will need to remind them often to "use your words," and you will need to provide the words for them to use until they master this skill. When they become frustrated, biting or hitting can often result. Before anyone gets hurt, tell a frustrated child to say, "I'm mad at you because you took my toy, and you should give it back to me," for example. Frequently, older children may not give younger children the opportunity to express themselves. You can model appropriate behavior by demonstrating patience and good communication skills by taking the time to listen to what small children have to say—no matter how long it takes.

Physical Touch

Some children and providers are more open to physical touch than others. Always be respectful of personal preferences and space when touching children. Touching children with affection usually elicits positive responses that can help them through challenging moments. Examples include physically guiding children to the table for a snack; gently taking their hands to pick up blocks and return them to the basket; patting their backs when they are tense or upset. Never physically punish children. The following are suggestions for responding to common behavioral challenges in family child care:

Inappropriate Language

When children use inappropriate words, tell them that you and the other children do not want to hear those words. Let them know that no one is allowed to use those words in your home. Make sure they understand that inappropriate language is inappropriate for everyone. Remember not to use inappropriate language in the presence of children, and be sure your family members know your expectations.

Temper Tantrums

When children have temper tantrums, remove them from the group. Place them in a safe, visible area in your home where they cannot hurt themselves. Pay as little attention to them as possible. Do not try to engage them in conversation when they are in the throes of a tantrum. After they calm down, pat their backs and talk about what happened. Encourage them to use words and give them other outlets for their feelings. Playing with water, pounding clay, or running outside are all good ways to burn off steam.

Biting

When children bite, take them aside and firmly say that biting hurts and is not allowed. Biting is serious. It causes many families to file formal complaints about their child care settings. If you have children in your program who have started biting, direct supervision is very important. Your ability to intervene quickly can prevent serious injury. Always encourage them to use words—provide words when the children do not know what to say. Look at your environment. Do you have sufficient toys and materials for everyone to use? How long do children have to wait to take their turn? Are you involved with the children? Are you accessible to them so that when their frustration begins to build, you are available to listen and help them?

Physical Aggression

When children hit or kick, tell them you understand they are angry, but they may not hit or kick, because it hurts others. Having a pillow available just for kicking can be helpful. One of the best ways to avoid hurtful behaviors is to keep children busy with large-motor activities and many opportunities for physical release. Again, your direct involvement with them cannot be overstated. Children are less likely to engage in hurtful behaviors when you are consistently interacting with them.

Not Participating

When children do not want to participate in a group activity, ask yourself if your activities are developmentally appropriate and interesting. What is the objective of the activity? Are there alternate ways to achieve your objective that may be more age appropriate and engaging for the children? During group time, invite the nonparticipants to sit next to you, pat their backs, give them something to hold or something to do, and thank them for participating.

If children do not participate because they are shy, do not force them to do something they don't want to do. Be patient and focus on their positive behaviors. Offer them activities and objects that interest them. Involve them in conversation and give them lots of support. Often when children are new to a program, they are slow to participate. Before a new child joins the group, talk to the other children about helping the new one feel welcome.

Whining

When children whine, pay as little attention as possible. Let them know you cannot understand what they are saying if they do not speak clearly. In some instances, children whine because they don't feel well. Make sure you are aware of any potential health problems that may affect them. Occasionally children whine because they feel apart from the other children in their group. Attempt to include all of them in ways that allow them to feel confident and successful.

Tattling

When children like to tattle, ignore their behavior as much as possible. In a family child care group, tattling is like a virus. If one child successfully gains attention by tattling, all the children will attempt to do the same. Give children special attention for all the positive things they do.

Nervous Habits

When children suck their fingers or exhibit other nervous habits, identify what else is going on then. Try to understand why they are worried or stressed. Distraction can be helpful—find something fun for them to do. Or give the child something to hold or keep their hands busy.

A Note about School Readiness

One of the unique aspects of family child care is the opportunity to have a child participate in your program from infancy to kindergarten. What wonderful opportunities can result from this type of continuity of care! When a provider incorporates curriculum objectives and applies them to each age group while periodically assessing the effectiveness of the curriculum, children benefit.

Opportunities for learning begin at birth. When parents and providers take advantage of all the opportunities for healthy growth and development, school readiness is simply a natural progression. For example, if toddlers are given ample opportunity to develop fine-motor skills by holding and using pencils, once they reach preschool stage, writing should not be a problem. If young children are exposed to books and sound recognition, the groundwork for reading has been established.

Providers who have preschoolers in their program have a special responsibility to make the transition from child care to school as easy and successful as possible. Most schools have established some basic requirements for entry into kindergarten programs. Find out what these requirements are in your area. Visit a local kindergarten class and speak with the teacher. Talk about the skills and characteristics that teachers find most useful for children entering school. Talk with parents about their goals and expectations for their children. Create good communication between yourself and the early education community in your area.

In preparing preschoolers, consider all of the skills necessary for young children to make a successful transition.

- Encourage children in your program to want to learn and go to school.
- Read aloud to children daily. This gives them a chance to learn about language, to enjoy the sound of your voice, and to be close to you.
- Set high standards and encourage children to try new things without intimidating them or belittling their fears.
- Listen to the children in your program to learn what's on their minds, what they know and don't know, and how they think and learn.
- Provide nutritious foods, safe places to play and learn, and a regular schedule.

- Show children how to get along with others, to share, and to take turns.
- Set a good example for the children in your program.
- Help children feel good about themselves and demonstrate that they can succeed.

Be generous with your support and encouragement. Always thank children for their efforts.

Assessment

In evaluating regulatory standards, many states have already included assessment requirements or are contemplating introducing assessment language. This poses an interesting challenge for many family child care providers.

Because family child care does not usually include groups containing six three-year-olds, the curriculum varies based on the ages and abilities of the various children enrolled in each program. As a result, assessment in family child care is more apt to be successful when a provider can clearly identify her specific developmental objectives for each child in care. Only then is it possible to determine whether your daily schedule of activities is actually promoting necessary skills and competencies for each child. One size does not fit all when it comes to curriculum. Individual goals need to be established, and each child's progress needs to be regularly evaluated for you to fairly assess the effectiveness of your program.

Another challenge you face when caring for mixed age groups, especially when infants are included, is that much of your time is spent in direct care. Tasks such as feeding children, changing diapers, and keeping your environment safe and clean are time consuming. The primary goal of this book is to help you understand that what you accomplish in the course of your day creates many teachable moments. Do not feel overwhelmed. You can maintain the character of your program and meet the regulatory requirements in your state. Periodic assessment of your daily schedule and its related activities along with how you meet the developmental needs of children in your own unique way will allow you to experience both satisfaction and success. There is really nothing new about wanting to meet healthy growth and development expectations. The majority of families and family child care providers have been meeting these expectations for many years. Don't be afraid to evaluate your program. Remember that you are teaching through the quality of your care.

The Importance of Play

It is easy to make the mistake of dismissing children's play as something inconsequential. We frequently use the term *child's play* to describe something that is easy or trivial. Anyone who has spent time with young children quickly realizes that is simply not true. When young children are playing, they are working. Play is the work of children. Children at play explore and practice new roles. They learn about a variety of materials, acquire social abilities, and learn to cope. They learn how and when to exercise their fantasies. Play helps children actively demonstrate what they feel and think about all the parts of their lives. Children take their play very seriously, and the opportunities for varied types of play are necessary in any quality family child care program.

In creating a daily schedule of activities that works effectively, you should look at the different types of play. Children, like adults, need downtime to relax. Some types of play provide that opportunity. Allowing children time to engage in play, whether independently or cooperatively, without structure and adult expectations, is a necessary component in a daily schedule for young children. Of course, it's possible to have too much unstructured time. This can be a problem in programs where there is little preplanning or not much thought given to curriculum. Children let you know if this is the case by becoming too loud, wound up, or withdrawn. Understanding individual temperaments and preferences will assist you in allotting an appropriate amount of time for free play.

Play allows children to rehearse events that may be difficult or anxiety producing. You can introduce types of play that prepare children for events they may find uncomfortable. For example, playing hospital, visiting a doctor's office, or moving from one home to another provide children with opportunities to address their fears about injury or change in a protected setting.

Physical play, such as handling a ball, promotes gross- and fine-motor skill development. Play that includes peekaboo or hide-and-seek helps young children feel assured that something can go away and come back again.

Pretending is a very important part of young children's play. Small children can feel big and in charge. They can take on roles that are not usually available to them. They try on different personalities and approaches to calling attention to themselves. Pretending allows children to work on their feelings about the world they live in.

If you closely observe children as they play, you will note that they can be very creative. Children in a supportive environment with the appropriate materials and tools will usually use their play to create positive learning experiences. When talking with children's families, you should reinforce your inclusion of opportunities for children to engage in play throughout the day. Explain how many of the teaching opportunities in your schedule are constructed to promote learning through games and interactive play.

The Power of Art

Why is art important in an early childhood program? First and foremost, young children love it. They are often fascinated to discover that the things they feel, sense, or want to express can be made visual by simply putting crayon to paper. Infants experience delight when they realize that the various marks on paper exist because of them. Art has the potential to enhance both intellectual and emotional growth in young children. In addition, physical development occurs in handling a crayon or brush and in dipping small fingers in paint and making marks on paper.

Art is important because it allows children to understand that people think and feel differently about the same things and that these differences are all right. Be sure that the children in your care understand there is not a right way to do art. One child may feel that painting an apple blue is appropriate. By encouraging the child who has painted the blue apple, you are reinforcing the concept of tolerance for different ideas and interpretations.

Art is important because it heightens children's awareness of the richness of their environment. They become more aware of colors, textures, shapes, and forms.

Art is also important because it helps children express their feelings without having to worry about being judged, as they would in conversation. Encourage young children to draw and talk about things that seem important to them emotionally. Very often, what appears to be a simple and routine drawing gives young children a great deal of satisfaction. Art can be a healthy release for children who feel tense or angry. Children who paint themselves as superheroes or fire chiefs are experiencing healthy self-realization. Art encourages children to think in original ways. For example, asking, "What would the world look like to a giant?" prompts children to respond creatively.

In thinking about all the positive development that can occur as the result of including art opportunities in your family child care setting, consider the following:

- Originality of ideas—avoid telling children what to draw.
- Independence—have all materials available so children can use them easily and independently when appropriate.
- Confidence in one's own abilities—encourage, encourage, encourage!
- Freedom to express personally meaningful ideas and feelings—try not to impose your judgment or value system on children's work.
- Acceptance of self as unique and valuable—acknowledge every attempt.
- Clarification of ideas and concepts—use art as an opportunity for discussion.

Reading with Children

The ability to understand the written word is an important skill for children to master. An early childhood curriculum is not generally designed to teach children how to read. Rather, it prepares them for learning how to read. Letter and sound recognition as well as broad exposure to books and other types of reading material should be included in your program. Have books, magazines, and papers around your home. Let the children in your program see that you like to read. Young children imitate what they see. The more you can demonstrate that reading is an activity preferable to watching television, for example, the more the children in your program will value the ability to read. If possible, use your local library frequently. Most libraries have incorporated some very creative programs for young children.

Demonstrate how reading is a necessary function of life. Don't restrict what you read aloud to children's books; read the labels on cans, map directions, and the print on the backs of cereal boxes to children. When outside, you can read signs, mailboxes, and other written material you and the children see.

At every stage of development, opportunities abound for introducing reading to children. You should have enough reading material for all the ages and stages of children in your program. Your collection of reading material should contain books to read to children and books for children to look at independently. When you arrange your space, remember that children should have quiet places to read or look at pictures. Introducing books enhances language, communication, and cognitive skills, eye-hand coordination, and the foundation for imaginative thinking. If you have school-age children enrolled in your program, encourage them to read to younger children and listen to them read their favorite stories. Imparting curiosity and a love of reading and storytelling to young children is a wondrous gift. When selecting books for young children, consider the following guidelines:

- Make sure children can handle the books. Books that are made of sturdy, heavier material, such as board books, are useful for infants and young toddlers.
- Books should have large, clear illustrations, which are more likely to capture children's attention.
- Books should tell inviting, pleasant stories. Examine books carefully for illustrations that might startle or frighten young children.

- Books that are filled with pictures of familiar objects help reinforce language development. Use the pictures to build children's vocabulary.

Infants and toddlers can be unintentionally destructive in their exploration; creating sturdy, colorful books that children can always have access to and can easily handle is a good idea. Choose materials that are sturdy and nontoxic for your pages. Choose pictures that are colorful and simple, and glue or paste them onto the book pages. It is especially fun to include photographs from your child care environment. Use a hole punch for the pages and cover, and attach them with brightly colored yarn. Older children in your program can help to create books for themselves and younger children. Make sure that your books are easily held by small hands.

Outdoor Play with Infants, Toddlers, and Preschool Children

Young children need to go outside on a daily basis. Infants, for instance, enjoy watching the patterns created by the sun and the feel of grass. Taking walks with a stroller is an appropriate way to take even the youngest children outside. Older children also benefit greatly by going outside on a daily basis. Connecting with nature and observing the changing seasons and weather patterns are invaluable experiences. Strollers, carriages, and infant seats can be very helpful when taking family child care groups outside. Some providers creatively use sleds and wagons.

Some providers find reasons not to take children outside. They complain that families do not send appropriate clothing to allow children to participate in outdoor activities. Or they say that by the time they get the children dressed and ready to go outside, someone invariably must go to the bathroom, and the whole long process begins again. Most licensed providers are required to take children outside daily. Good organization is key to implementing this requirement.

Children who are allowed to run and play outside burn off excess energy and usually have better appetites, rest better, and in most cases have better dispositions than children who are kept indoors. You can incorporate creative activities that include large-motor skills, science, and sensory activities, such as water and sand and art activities, that may not be easily implemented inside your home. Keeping older children inside because you are not prepared to bring participating infants outside is not appropriate. It is important to have good communication about your expectations with all your families when they enroll their children. They need to understand your policy and obligation to take all the children outside daily.

Your daily schedule should include a routine of outdoor play that works for you as well as the children. Timing of snacks, bathroom breaks, and outdoor play is entirely up to you. Encourage and provide ample opportunity for age-appropriate self-help skills, such as putting on jackets and sweaters. This allows you to focus on dressing infants and toddlers.

You are in a position to develop a daily schedule that works for you as well as all the children in your care. Determine snacktime and bathroom breaks in relation to your scheduled outdoor play. Encourage and provide ample opportunity for children to develop age-appropriate self-help skills, such as taking jackets on and off. This not only meets developmental objectives, but it enhances your ability to prepare all of the children for outdoor play in an organized fashion.

It is helpful to remember that much of how you teach is through your good example. Demonstrate your enjoyment of the outdoors. If children feel because of what you demonstrate that going outside is just too much of a bother, or there is really nothing fun to do outside, you are denying them wonderful and free learning experiences. Organize your daily schedule in a way that accommodates outdoor play in a positive way, even when you are caring for a diverse group of children. The following section on outdoor group games has been included to give you some ideas regarding outside play.

Group Games

Regardless of how structured your curriculum is, children need daily opportunities for physical activity. A portion of each day should be allotted for large-motor activity. The games described here were developed to maximize participation and minimize failure. Playing games has the advantage of involving providers, as well as allowing children to develop varied and complementary skills.

Children enjoy and benefit from organized games. While older children are playing games with rules, have younger children involved in a separate activity that allows you to supervise all the children simultaneously. It is never a good idea to have younger children inside napping, for example, while you are outside with other children. Infants may not be able to participate in organized games, but they can certainly benefit from observing the older children playing. Give toddlers the opportunity to play in organized games when appropriate. Look for creative ways to involve them or adapt a game in a way that allows toddlers to play a simpler "down-sized" version. Help ensure the success of the games by explaining them before the children begin. This will help the children understand the rules and increase their excitement.

- Choose games that will accommodate the majority of children.
- Know the game before teaching it to the children.
- Make sure all the children are within your sight, and encourage all the children who can to participate.
- It is never a good idea to have young children standing in one place for too long. Position them when you are ready to begin.
- Establish boundaries and identify safety hazards. If you are playing in a public area, such as a park, make sure you are aware of potential hazards prior to playing.
- Present the rules of the game in sequence. Say each step out loud and demonstrate each step when possible. Remember, you can alter or simplify games so they are fun for all the children in your program rather than introducing a game that is too overwhelming. In the beginning, keep the rules simple. Be brief and to the point.
- Don't force children to play. Involve as many children as possible, and if the games are fun, you will find that eventually everyone will want to play.

No Touch

Developmental Goal: No-Touch supports children's control of their bodies and reinforces balance and coordination.

Equipment: None

Game Play: On a start signal, all the players move about within a designated area. The goal is to try to move about without touching one another. If a player bumps or touches another player, both stop, stand back to back, and count to ten. They may then return to the game.

Tips:

- Start with a large play area and progressively decrease its size.
- As the children develop skill in moving without bumping into one another, have them hop or skip while playing the game.

The Boss

Developmental Goal: This game helps children develop finger manipulations as well as eye-hand coordination. It is a fun game that stimulates the imagination.

Equipment: An easy to hold object, such as a ball or beanbag. Avoid anything that may become a choking hazard.

Game Play: Have the children sit in a circle. Give one child the object to hold. When you give the start signal, have the children quickly pass the object around the circle without dropping it. If the object is dropped, the child who dropped it must pick it up and pass it on to the next child. When the signal to stop is given, the child with the object in his or her hands is The Boss. No stigma is attached to being caught with an object, because every player will eventually be The Boss.

Tips:

- The signal to start and stop can be musical.
- Have the player caught with the object in his or her hands go to the middle of the circle and perform a task, such as five jumping jacks.

Color Mix

Developmental Goal: Color Mix helps children develop coordination and learn to identify colors.

Equipment: A different colored spot for each player — a variety of poly spots or construction paper

Game Preparation: Arrange colored spots in a large circle. You will need one for each child except the one who is It.

Game Play: All players but the one who is It stand on a colored spot. The child who is It stands in the middle of the circle. As you call out two or more colors, those on the colors must trade places. As the exchange is being made, It attempts to take a color place. The player not landing on a color spot is It.

Tips:

- When children are ready for a challenge, call out "Spill the paint" so that everyone in the circle looks for a new spot.
- Have children color or paint paper to make the spots. This is a great way to introduce increased color recognition.

Mousetrap

Developmental Goal: Along with being fun, this game helps children develop agility.

Equipment: None

Game Play: Divide players into two groups. One group holds hands in a circle to represent the mousetrap, while the other group, the mice, scatter around the outside of the circle. One player is It. It stands with her back to the mousetrap. When It says "Open!" the children in the circle raise their arms, opening the mousetrap. The mice then run in and out of the circle as often as they dare. When It says "Close!" the children lower their arms, closing the mousetrap. Any mice caught inside then join the mousetrap circle. Switch groups and begin again.

Tip: Designate a time limit or number of turns for each group. When the time is up, congratulate those who were not caught.

Spaceship

Developmental Goal: Spaceship allows children to run, start, and stop on a signal.

Equipment: None

Game Play: Arrange players evenly in a circle about 5 feet across. Assign each player a spaceship name, such as *Nautilus, Jupiter, Mercury, Saturn,* and *Explorer.* Stand in the middle of the circle. Tell the children you represent Earth. As you call out the name of one of the spaceships, that child will begin running around the circle (orbiting Earth). They should keep running until you call "Touchdown!" At that point, the children must cut through the circle, run to and tag your outstretched hand, and then run back to their starting spots. You can then call a new spaceship.

Tips:

- Caution runners to slow down before reaching you.
- If you keep children moving at a fast pace, they won't have to wait long for new turns. Young children love to run, so their enthusiasm will be high.
- When the children are ready for a new challenge, call more than one spaceship at a time.

Little Bear

Developmental Goal: Little Bear supports coordination.

Equipment: None

Game Play: Have the children spread out in a wide, clear space. Choose a player to be Little Bear. Little Bear calls, "Who's afraid of the Little Bear?" The other children answer "Not me!" Little Bear demands that the children skip. Also skipping, Little Bear tags as many children as possible. Players who are tagged become Little Bear's helpers.

Tips:

- When all the players have been tagged, select a new Little Bear and repeat the game.

- Little Bear may demand walking, running, galloping, hopping, jumping, or sliding. You can also be creative and add other choices, such as driving or flying. Little Bear and his helpers must use the same skills.

Martians

Developmental Goal: This game develops speed and agility and is a fun way to review colors.

Equipment: None

Game Play: Choose one player to be the Martian, who stands in the middle of the play area. The other children are Earthlings. They must stand facing the Martian. The Earthlings chant, "Martian, Martian, will you take us to the stars?" The Martian replies "Yes, if you are wearing [name any color]." Earthlings wearing that color may walk safely across the space. The remaining Earthlings run across, trying to reach the other side safely. Any Earthling tagged by the Martian must join him and help catch the other Earthlings.

Tips:

- It's helpful to explain that Martians come from the planet Mars so the word makes sense to the children.
- Depending on the size of the group, when there are only a few Earthlings left, select a new Martian and repeat the game.

Busy Bee Tag

Developmental Goal: Busy Bee Tag reinforces children's spatial awareness skills, listening skills, and coordination.

Equipment: None

Game Play: When you call the signal "Busy Bee," all of the children move into the designated space. As players are moving, call out various directions, such as "back to back" and "knee to foot." In response to the body parts you name, players pair up with the person closest to them and touch those body parts together. Let the children hold their positions for a few seconds; then call "Busy Bee" and repeat the process.

Tips:

- Allow the players to use their creativity to accomplish the task you call out. You will see a variety of correct responses.
- It is also possible to play this game inside.

Whistle Mixer

Developmental Goal: This activity supports the development of memory skills.

Equipment: Whistle

Game Play: Have the players scatter throughout the play area. Assign different instructions to each number of whistle-blows. For example, one blow may mean everyone should freeze, two blows mean players have five seconds to find a partner, etc. When you give the start signal, all players begin moving around the play area. After the players move for ten to fifteen seconds, blow the whistle. When the players have properly responded to the whistle signal, repeat the procedure using a different signal.

Tips:

- It is best to limit the number of signals to five.
- Use a drum, tambourine, or hand claps to signal.
- Assign different commands, such as skipping, jumping, or hopping on one foot, for the signals.

Back-to-Back Get Up

Developmental Goal: This game encourages cooperation.

Equipment: None

Game Play: Have children pair off and stand back to back. Each pair hooks elbows and sits down cooperatively by pressing their backs together. From a sitting position, they should move their feet close to their bottoms and stand back up as a unit.

Tip: Try it without hooking elbows — no hands!

Caterpillar

Developmental Goal: Caterpillar supports coordination and cooperation.

Equipment: Simple obstacle course

Game Play: Players line up, one behind the other with their hands on the ankles of the person in front of them. Instruct the players to move forward as a group.

Tip: Younger children can play this game while holding on to the waist of the person in front.

Frantic Balloon

Developmental Goal: Participate in cooperative play.

Equipment: One balloon for every two players and a stopwatch

Game Play: Scatter the players throughout the play area and give half of them balloons. On the signal "Go," start the stopwatch. All players with balloons tap them into the air, using any part of their bodies. Then all the players work together to keep the balloons off the ground. No balloon can be caught at any time, and nobody can hit the same balloon twice in a row.

Tips:

- If a balloon hits the ground, the player can pick it up and keep playing.
- Children can also hold hands with a partner.

Learning from Mistakes Others Have Made

It is useful to examine examples of worst as well as best practices. Often there is no conscious intent on the part of the provider—only a lack of understanding. In other instances, the provider may be overwhelmed financially or organizationally and unable to make appropriate decisions. In looking at the following examples, remember that in each one of these anecdotes, the behavior described should never occur in a family child care environment.

Infants

When I asked to see the napping children during a home visit, I was taken into a darkened room. When I looked into the crib to see the sleeping infant, much to my surprise I found an infant sleeping with numerous cats! The unlicensed provider could not understand why I was so upset. **Never allow pets to sleep in the same napping facility as a sleeping child.**

I received a complaint alleging that a provider had left an infant in a soiled diaper for most of a day, resulting in the baby's bottom becoming red and raw. The infant had to be taken to the hospital for outpatient treatment. When I arrived at the provider's home—a lovely home, I might add—I fully expected the provider to deny the allegation. Much to my surprise, she readily admitted she had left the baby in the soiled diaper. She proudly explained to me that she had warned the mother about not leaving sufficient diapers and she had finally taught the mother "a good lesson." **Never, ever use a child to retaliate against a parent.**

Toddlers

I once encountered a provider who tied toddlers to their potty chairs after each meal and snack. What I found most amazing was the absolute confidence she felt in her practice of training toddlers. When interviewing parents of children enrolled in that program, I discovered that many of them admitted knowing about this practice and approving of it. One parent explained to me, "The provider was saving him from the responsibility of toilet training and he was grateful for it." **Do not compromise the safety or well-being of a child, even if a parent has no objection or requests that you do something you know is inappropriate.**

I once received a complaint from a father who went to a provider's home to pick up his child and found his toddler locked in the provider's van, beating hysterically at the doors to get out. When the irate father confronted the provider, child in hand, she calmly told him she hadn't realized the child wasn't in the house with the other children. She indicated she must have left him in the van when picking up some of the other children two hours before. When I arrived to investigate, the provider informed me that she should have known the toddler was missing because her program was too quiet. **Toddlers require a great amount of supervision and attention. If you are not up to the challenge, do not provide child care for toddlers.**

Preschool Children

Once, while conducting an unannounced visit, I heard an infant crying in an unlicensed area of a provider's home. When I questioned the provider about the infant, she denied that any other children were present, because an additional child would mean she was overenrolled. I could hear the infant crying, and I knew the provider also heard the infant crying. There we were, in spite of the cry of the infant, debating the issue back and forth. In an attempt to convince me I was mistaken, the provider looked down at a preschool child who was standing nearby and said, "We can't have snack until the licensor leaves—please tell her there are no other babies here." The poor child appeared so confused; it was obvious the provider had placed him in a terrible position. **Never coerce or bribe a child to lie or involve a child in a deceit. Do not care for more children than you are licensed for.**

On one occasion, I visited a home where the provider was offering family child care in addition to providing foster care. As soon as I arrived, she indicated that she was having an awful day. She immediately began a chronology of events that centered on one little boy. She proceeded to tell me about how wonderfully all the other children in her home behaved except for this one child. As if that weren't bad enough, she began a sordid history about the child's mother. All this while the child was standing two feet from her side. To this day, I cannot forget the look of hurt in that little boy's eyes. **Never ridicule, humiliate, denigrate, or embarrass a child in your care.**

Transporting Children

Transporting family child care children in your vehicle should require a great deal of consideration on your part. When determining if field trips, errands, or transporting children from their homes or schools will be a normal or regularly scheduled activity, it is a good idea to check with your insurance company for any special liability provisions you are required to meet. Families should be aware of your schedule, and they should know when and how frequently children are not at the child care home. Do not put yourself in a situation where a parent or family member arrives to pick up a child only to find an empty house and no knowledge of where you and the children have gone. Make sure you have written permission to take the enrolled children in your vehicle—it is a good idea to update those signed permissions yearly.

Always drive safely: obey speed limits, do not run red lights or stop signs, and do not talk on a cell phone or send a text message while driving. Be a defensive driver and remember that you are responsible for not only your safety but the safety of the children you have been entrusted to care for as well. Double check that the children are always secured appropriately in their seats. If you are using car or booster seats, make sure these devices have been installed properly. Be sure to understand all the required regulatory and legal expectations when transporting enrolled children.

Car Accidents

If a car accident occurs while transporting children in your program:

- **Be aware of your surroundings.** Make sure you are not in the path of oncoming traffic. If you are able, pull off to the side of the road. Don't get out unless absolutely necessary, and make sure all of the children are secured in their seats.
- **Turn off your ignition.** Turning off the ignition will reduce the risk of fire. Turn on your hazard lights so other drivers can see you.
- **Get help!** If you have a cell phone (which is a good idea!), call 911. Tell the person answering the call that you are transporting children.
- **Check everyone for injuries.** Don't move any of the children unless they are in further danger. If you must move a child out of the car, try to remove the entire safety seat with the child still strapped in. Remove children from the side of the vehicle away from the road when possible.

- **Gather information.** It is always advisable to gather information if another individual(s) are involved in the accident; however, your primary responsibility is to directly supervise all the children and to assure their safety and well-being.

- **Carry emergency information for each child transported.** You should carry a bag or a container with emergency information for all the children you transport. Include signed parental permission slips that allow for immediate medical treatment. Contact the parents or guardians as soon as possible. In many states, licensing requirements stipulate that you must notify parents, guardians, and your licensing authority of any accidents or injuries that involve participating children. Know and understand those regulations as well as any relevant time lines for notification.

- **Use comforting words.** Explain what happened: "We've been in an accident, and people are going to come to help us." Ask if the children feel pain anywhere, and tell them a doctor will help them feel better soon.

- **Stay still.** In most cases, you should not move injured children without professional help. Challenge them to stay as still as possible until paramedics arrive and evaluate their injuries. Although neck or back pain most commonly indicates a minor strain, all pain should be treated seriously, as it could be from spinal cord injuries or fractures.

- **Control bleeding.** Apply direct, firm pressure to any obvious wounds with a clean shirt or a towel. If children can hold a bandage in place, ask them to.

- **Stay calm.** Children will follow your example.

Computers: For You and the Children

A computer in your family child care environment benefits children and can be of great benefit to you. Consider the following:

- Many states are now offering updated regulatory and policy information online.
- Many online training opportunities are available to providers. These help you to stay current and work around your busy and often long schedule.
- Many Web sites are now available for family child care providers to network and share information. These can assist you in what can be a very isolating profession.

What Can Children Learn from Computers?

These are a few of the skills and traits children can develop as they work and play with computers:

- thinking skills
- problem solving
- comprehension
- eye-hand coordination
- visual memory
- decision making
- number and letter skills
- following directions
- increased attention span
- positive attitude toward computers
- independence and confidence
- social skills

Above all, computers help children feel as if they are a part of the world of grown-ups. Computers are fun!

Choosing Appropriate Software

The value of computers rests primarily on the software installed. You should try out software whenever possible to see if it will achieve your goals and if it appeals to the children in your care. Here are other factors to consider when selecting software:

- Is it appropriate for the ages and abilities of the children?
- What concepts and skills does it teach?
- Do children become actively involved in the game or program?
- Are the directions clear?
- Can children operate this program independently?
- Does it provide for increased complexity?
- Does it offer positive reinforcement?
- What happens if the child makes a mistake?
- Is it fun enough to keep children interested?

A computer can support many learning areas. Make sure your computer is in a safe location and that all equipment is positioned securely. Place the computer so that older children can easily use it, while keeping it inaccessible to mobile infants and curious toddlers unless you assist them.

Custody Issues

You may have an enrolled child whose parents are divorcing or separating and are attempting to work out formal custody arrangements or a child from a single-parent family. Suddenly a stranger who identifies himself as the other parent arrives at the child care home demanding to see the child.

Parents, guardians, and providers need to understand that a provider cannot legally take the word of one parent over another about who has access to a child during child care hours. If custody has been established by a court, make sure you have a copy of the legal papers and follow its directions. If there is a restraining order in place, a copy of it must be included in the child's file. In the majority of states, before a court has made a ruling, both parents have equal rights regardless of which parent is paying for child care or which parent signed the child care contract.

Two online publications with helpful information are

- *Releasing Children from Child Care and Custody Issues: With Whom Can the Child Go Home?* http://www.childcarelaw.org/docs/releasingchildren.pdf
- *Guidelines for Releasing Children and Custody Issues* http://www.publiccounsel .org/publications/release.pdf

Pets in Your Home

Having a business in your home usually means that everyone shares common space. How does this commingling affect the family pet? Dog bites are a very common health risk for young children, especially during the summer months. The majority of children bitten are bitten by dogs they know, and while German shepherds and Doberman pinschers are often assumed to be the breeds that bite most often, any dog can attack if provoked. Here are some suggestions to protect children in your care.

- Children should be at least five years old before spending time with your family dog so they can understand how to treat it gently. If the children in your program are under five, keep your dog in a separate area of your home or yard away from the children.
- Never leave a child near a dog without adult supervision, even when you are convinced your dog is good with children.
- Instruct children in your program to stand completely still if a dog growls at or chases them.
- Teach children when playing with dogs never to pull tails or run past or disturb them while they are eating or chewing on a toy or bone.
- Teach children to always allow their closed fist to be sniffed before reaching out to pet the dog.

If you are unsure about the safety and healthy inclusion of other pets, contact your local public health department. Pets like lizards, turtles, parrots, and ferrets can create health problems and are not recommended in early child care settings. Cat fur can be the source of allergic reactions, and exposure to kitty litter is certainly not appropriate. Do your homework. Children can learn about animals through positive experiences that may or may not include pets. Your responsibility to protect children from harm is your number one priority. Thoroughly investigate the appropriateness of any pet or animal you choose to introduce to the children you care for.

Food Allergies

You have a very real responsibility in regard to the foods you obtain and prepare. While this is true for all children, it may mean life or death for children with food allergies. It is important that you are asking and receiving all the pertinent information you need when enrolling a child in your program. Ask each child's family about any known food allergies. If you are given information you do not understand, ask for more information or request information from the child's doctor.

As of January 2006, federal law requires all major allergens to be clearly listed on labels. Know what you are buying. If a family has identified a child's food allergy, do not buy food products that contain that substance even if you have served that food to that child in the past with no negative consequences.

If families are unaware of a food allergy and you notice that a child develops symptoms after being exposed to certain foods while in your care, notify the child's family at once. These symptoms can include but are not limited to hives, rashes, swollen tongue or lips, or difficulty breathing. If symptoms begin, start a diary in collaboration with the child's family for a few weeks to record what foods the child has been eating, especially anything newly introduced.

Communicate frequently with families and share any observations that may be different or in addition to what they have shared with you. Remember that information is important, and once you have been given relevant information about a child's food allergy, you incur a potential liability if you do not take all the precautions necessary to keep that child safe.

Water Safety

Drowning is one of the leading causes of death among young children. A small child can drown in less than one inch of water. Whenever you allow children to play with or near water tubs, swimming pools, wading pools, bathtubs, ponds, streams, or marshes, you must be in direct and constant supervision. Most states have specific regulatory language regarding safety requirements governing your program. Know and understand what those requirements include. It is a good idea to always have signed permission forms from families if you intend to use a swimming pool during child care hours.

Some providers include swimming instruction as part of their curriculum. It is important for the welfare of all the children in care that you teach children basic safety rules. Here are examples of some rules that need to be followed when using a pool during child care hours:

- Swim or play in the water only when an adult has been identified to watch you.
- Do not run, push, or dunk in or around water.
- Do not bring glass near the area.
- Do not swim with something in your mouth.
- Yell for help only when you need it.

All adults supervising children during water play should know how to administer mouth-to-mouth resuscitation, the technique to restore breathing.

Product Safety

Faulty equipment can pose a very real hazard in a family child care home because so much of the equipment used is often obtained as gifts or purchased at yard sales or resale shops. Among children under four years of age, unintentional injuries, such as drowning, suffocation, and choking, remain leading causes of accidental death. Far too many of these deaths occur when children are placed in products intended to protect them from harm, such as cradles, cribs, or bath seats.

Deaths of children in family child care homes because of product failures have sadly occurred. Many of these deaths were the result of strangulation or suffocation caused by faulty equipment. Proving a death resulted from faulty equipment can be an expensive and uphill battle. Understanding product liability, protecting your business, and most important, assuring the safety of the children in your program must be primary concerns when obtaining materials and equipment.

Do not rely solely on a manufacturer's Web site for recall information. The U.S. Consumer Product Safety Commission (CPSC) is currently advocating for manufacturers to post all recall information on the manufacturer's Web site. Currently, many companies that post recall information do not always post updated or complete lists. There is an additional problem in the fact that a product may have accumulated reported incidents, including deaths, without the product being placed on a recall list at the time you make your inquiry. If you have acquired a piece of equipment and would like to find out if incidents have been reported, CPSC will send you detailed information. If you need information on more than one brand, send a separate letter for each brand. The following Web sites are good places to search for reliable child safety information:

- American Academy of Pediatrics: www.aap.org
- Safe Kids USA: www.safekids.org
- U.S. Consumer Product Safety Commission: www.cpsc.gov
- The Consumer Federation of America: www.consumerfed.org
- National Highway Traffic Safety Administration (for car seat recommendations and installation): www.nhtsa.dot.gov

Manufacturers have a responsibility to notify consumers who have submitted registration cards if that product is recalled. If the equipment was not purchased new and you do not have a manufacturer's registration card, you can create one and mail it to the company.

Sample Product Registration Card:

Your Name: _____

Telephone Number: _____

Address: _____

City: _____ State: _____

Zip Code: _____

Product Brand Manufacturer: _____

Product Model Number: _____

Signature and Date: _____

Don't forget to photocopy the registration card and keep the copy in your files.

Emergency Evacuations

It is not possible to offer quality child care without first considering the health and safety of all the enrolled children. Providers must realistically assess their ability to evacuate all participating children simultaneously. You always need to be prepared for an emergency, such as a fire or a natural disaster. In the case of family child care programs, which usually include children of various ages and abilities, having a plan in place is critical, as the following story will attest.

A licensed family child care provider's home burned to the ground one winter's night. It was a lovely home, and the provider was understandably devastated. The firefighters had determined that the blaze started in a stack of napping mats that had been stored too closely to a radiator. They speculated the mats could have been smoldering for hours before they finally ignited. The provider shared how heartbroken she felt because the wood framed home had burned so quickly they were unable to get their personal possessions out. She was grateful, however, that she and her family had escaped without injury. She was also grateful that the fire had occurred after the child care children had left for the day. In looking at what was left of her home, it was easy to understand exactly what she was trying to say. Although this provider was licensed and had approved space on her basement level with the appropriate number of exits and the required smoke detectors, it was difficult to imagine how she could have safely evacuated six small children, including two infants, who were enrolled in her program and had attended earlier that day. It was one thing to discuss what might occur in the event of a fire and another to actually look at what had occurred as the result of a fire.

In caring for small children, it is critically important that you be prepared for an emergency. You need to know how you are going to get all of the children out of your home as quickly and safely as possible. This includes the infants who are not walking, the toddlers who are unsteady on their feet, and the preschool age children who are apt to panic and hide or run ahead into a dangerous situation. As a family child care provider, you need to have an appropriate evacuation plan in place, and you and the children need to practice, practice, practice. You need to practice your evacuation from every area of your home where you provide child care. You need to practice when children are napping and when they are having lunch. The more frequently you practice evacuation, the more proficient children will be in the event of an emergency. Some providers have many excuses for not practicing evacuation: it's too cold, the children aren't feeling well, I'm on the second floor, I have infants in care. If an emergency occurs, it is important to remember that not one of those factors will stop your home from being harmed.

Practice makes perfect. With practice, the smallest children immediately and calmly line up at an exit when a provider sets off her smoke detector. Practicing evacuation at a minimum of once a month is an important part of any provider's curriculum. It will help children recognize the sound of the smoke alarm and respond accordingly. Practicing in all types of weather conditions allows you to accommodate changes in where your outside meeting place will be. Working smoke detectors are not only a basic necessity, but in most states a regulatory requirement. Make sure your smoke detectors are well maintained. A working smoke detector can quite literally mean the difference between life and death. Many states are now requiring carbon monoxide detectors as well.

Finally, if you care for infants, your evacuation plan should include special considerations. For example, do you have a crib with castors that you can use to transport infants while escorting the other children from your home? Where are your infants napping in relation to your exits?

Think about how you will get out safely with all your children in tow. Remember that with practice, even the smallest child can respond quickly and efficiently.

Additional Resources
Books

Allen, K. Eileen, and Lynn R. Marotz. 1989. *Developmental Profiles Birth to Six.* Albany, NY: Delmar.

Brazelton, T. Berry, 1974. *Toddlers and Parents.* New York: Dell.

Cherry, Clare. 1983. *Please Don't Sit on the Kids: Alternatives to Punitive Discipline.* Belmont, CA: David S. Lake.

Copeland, Tom 1999. *Family Child Care Marketing Guide: How to Build Enrollment and Promote Your Business as a Child Care.* St. Paul: Redleaf Press.

———. 2004. *Family Child Care Legal and Insurance Guide: How to Reduce the Risks of Running Your Business.* St. Paul: Redleaf Press.

———. 2006. *Family Child Care Contracts and Policies: How to Be Businesslike in a Caring Profession.* 3rd ed. St. Paul: Redleaf Press.

———. 2009. *Family Child Care Business Planning Guide.* St. Paul: Redleaf Press.

———. 2009. *Family Child Care Money Management and Retirement Guide.* St. Paul: Redleaf Press.

Copple, Carol, and Sue Bredekamp. 2009. *Developmentally Appropriate Practice in Early Childhood Programs Serving Children from Birth through Age 8.* 3rd ed. Washington, DC: National Association for the Education of Young Children.

Croft, Doreen J., and Robert D. Hess. 1985. *An Activities Handbook for Teachers of Young Children.* Boston: Houghton Mifflin.

Darling-Kuria, Nikki. 2010. *Brain-Based Early Learning.* St. Paul: Redleaf Press.

Denham, Susanne A. 1988. *Emotional Development in Young Children.* New York: The Guilford Press.

Dennis, Kirsten, and Tressa Azpiri. 2005. *Sign to Learn: American Sign Language in the Early Childhood Classroom.* St. Paul: Redleaf Press.

Felcher, E. Marla. 2001. *It's No Accident.* Monroe, ME: Common Courage Press.

Flemming, Bonnie Mack, Darlene Softly Hamilton, and JoAnne Deal Hicks. 1977. *Resources for Creative Teaching in Early Childhood.* San Diego: Harcourt Brace Jovanovich.

Hildebrand, Verna. 1981. *Introduction to Early Childhood Education.* New York: Macmillan.

Hymes, James L. 1981. *Teaching the Child under Six.* Columbus, OH: Merrill.

Johnson, Jeff A. 2006. *Do-It-Yourself Early Learning.* St. Paul: Redleaf Press.

———. 2007. *Finding Your Smile Again.* St. Paul: Redleaf Press.

———. 2008. *Everyday Early Learning.* St. Paul: Redleaf Press.

———. 2010. *Keeping Your Smile.* St. Paul: Redleaf Press.

Keyser, Janis. 2006. *From Parents to Partners.* St. Paul: Redleaf Press.

Miller, Karen. 1985. *Ages and Stages.* Marshfield, MA: Telshare.

———. 1989. *The Outside Play and Learning Book.* Mt. Rainier, MD: Gryphon House.

Mooney, Carol. 2000. *Theories of Childhood: An Introduction to Dewey, Montessori, Erikson, Piaget, and Vygotsky.* St. Paul: Redleaf Press.

———. 2010. *Theories of Attachment: An Introduction to Bowlby, Ainsworth, Gerber, Brazelton, Kennell, and Klaus.* St. Paul: Redleaf Press.

Petty, Karen. 2010. *Developmental Milestones of Young Children.* St. Paul: Redleaf Press.

Powers, Julie. 2005: *Parent-Friendly Early Learning.* St. Paul: Redleaf Press.

Redleaf, Rhoda. 2009. *Hey Kids! Out the Door, Let's Explore!* St. Paul: Redleaf Press.

Salkind, Neil J., and Sueann Robinson Ambron. 1987. *Child Development.* New York: Holt, Rinehart and Winston.

Smith, Connie Jo. 2008. *Behavioral Challenges in Early Childhood Settings.* St. Paul: Redleaf Press.

Tarrow, Nora Bernstein, and Sara Wynn Lundsteen. 1981. *Activities and Resources for Guiding Young Children's Learning.* New York: McGraw-Hill.

Web Sites

About.com

www.childcare.about.com

This Web site provides tips and advice for families seeking child care and addresses questions about safety, cost, and behavior. It also provides some fun activities to inspire parents and child care providers alike.

American Academy of Pediatrics

www.healthychildcare.org

For families who are looking for more than just child care advice and resources, this site also provides pediatricians' advice and information about health practice standards in early childhood settings.

ChildCare.gov

www.childcare.gov

This is a government-sponsored Web site that provides information about government-based child care for parents and providers. It includes legal information about regulations, licensing, and more.

Child Care & Early Education Research Connections

http://www.researchconnections.org/childcare/welcome;jsessionid=9F1056237DB37F061700E7A4422632AC

Research Connections provides a database of the latest research on early education and child care for researchers, policy makers, and practitioners.

National Association of Child Care Resource & Referral Agencies (NACCRRA)

www.naccrra.org

This is the Web site of an agency whose mission is to ensure affordable child care for children all over the United States. It provides published data, training manuals, articles, and basic information on receiving and implementing the best child care practices in your area.

National Association for the Education of Young Children (NAEYC)

www.naeyc.org

The NAEYC is one the nation's leading child care organizations and is dedicated to improving the well-being of young children and the quality of early education. Its Web site provides information about upcoming conferences, child care resources, publications, and membership.

National Association for Family Child Care

www.nafcc.org

This nonprofit organization is committed to strengthening state and local associations as the primary supports for child care providers. It holds conferences, offers training, and provides information on public policy, business practices, and resources for parents.

National Institute of Child Health and Human Development

www.nichd.nih.gov

This institute is dedicated to supporting research on health topics related to children, adults, and families, addressing topics such as infertility, growth and development, and preventing birth defects.

Index